The

AMA

AMERICAN MANAGEMENT ASSOCIATION

Style
Guide
for
Business
Writing

The

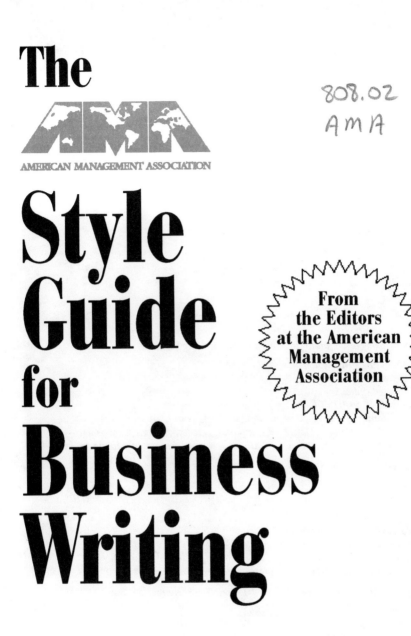

AMERICAN MANAGEMENT ASSOCIATION

Style Guide for Business Writing

From
the Editors
at the American
Management
Association

amacom
American Management Association

New York • Boston • Chicago • Kansas City • San Francisco • Washington, D.C.
Brussels • Mexico City • Tokyo • Toronto

This publication is designed to provide accurate and authoritative information in regard to the subject matter covered. It is sold with the understanding that the publisher is not engaged in rendering legal, accounting, or other professional service. If legal advice or other expert assistance is required, the services of a competent professional person should be sought.

Library of Congress Cataloging-in-Publication Data

The AMA style guide for business writing.
    p.   cm.
    Includes index.
    ISBN 0-8144-0297-6
    1. Commercial correspondence—Handbooks, manuals, etc.
    2. Business writing—Handbooks, manuals, etc.   3. English language—Business English—Handbooks, manuals, etc.   I. American Management Association.
    HF5726.A49   1996
    808'.06665—dc20   *96-4138*
                                                          CIP

Printing number

10 9 8 7 6 5 4 3 2 1

CONTENTS

INTRODUCTION

The AMA Style Guide for Business Writing is designed specifically for business managers. As its editors, we recognize that the English language is dynamic and changing. No precise style is permanent, and, as trends develop, usage and acceptable rules of communication change. This book should be thought of as a collection of guidelines rather than as strict rules that never change or vary.

We also recognize that as a manager, you need to communicate clearly and precisely. Whether that communication occurs through reports and memos, letters, speeches, or verbally, the precision in your use of the language determines how clearly your message is received. This style guide is aimed at you because precision and clarity in communication are essential to you and your success. Our purpose is to provide an easy-to-use and comprehensive guide to style and clarity in communication. One of the most important realities of business life is that you are judged by how well you adhere to the standards of communication. When questions arise, for example, about the correct method for footnoting a source in a business report, you can refer to the *AMA Style Guide* as an authoritative source for the right information.

The Guide is arranged alphabetically. Check the Table of Contents for the range of topics. You may also flip through the book to find the topic of interest to you. Many sections end with cross-references to other related sections. If you do not find the topic you are looking for, check the detailed index at the back of the book.

Many topics cover extremely basic principles of style. The experienced manager may find these sections useful in providing guidelines to less experienced employees or in determining questions of style not addressed for many years. Some topics in this book will not be in agreement with similar subject matter found in other style guides. The preferred usage we present will help you to make informed judgments about how to best express yourself to others. Using the style guide will enable you to communicate with consistency, clarity, and precision—our primary aim.

ABBREVIATIONS

An abbreviation is a form of shorthand, enabling readers to understand the meaning of a word or phrase without needing to see it written out in full. Abbreviations may take the form of letters to represent a longer organization or agency name or a few letters used to represent a longer word. Use consistent and universally accepted forms of abbreviations for common words.

1. Know when to use abbreviations.

In most formal business writing, do not abbreviate mathematical symbols, numbers, days of the week, or months when used in sentences. These may be abbreviated in technical writing, financial reports, and graphic presentations, however.

Incorrect:
The deadline is the 3rd Wed. in Oct.

Correct:
The deadline is the third Wednesday in October.

Informal writing, including brief memos and notes, may include abbreviations of many terms, with few rules except one: The meaning should always be clear.

Unacceptable owing to lack of clarity:
D.L.—3rd W./10.

Acceptable in informal writing:
The deadline is the 3rd Wed. in Oct.

Abbreviations for units of measurement should never be used unless in combination with a numeric value, and never if the number is spelled out.

Incorrect:

The current budget covers a three-mo. period.
A budget is broken down by mo. and yr.
The $ amount of the budget has been approved.
How many in. long is your desk?

Correct:

The current budget covers a three-month period.
A budget is broken down by month and year.
Our $6,000 expense budget has been approved.
There is room for a 60-in. desk.

2. Know when to use periods with abbreviations.

When abbreviating the names of organizations or agencies, do not use periods.

Incorrect:

I.R.S.	A.M.A.	N.Y.C.
A.B.C.	M.M.M.	T.S.E.

Correct:

IRS	AMA	NYC
ABC	MMM	TSE

In technical writing, omit periods after most abbreviations of units of measurement, except *no.* and *in.* (because they have entirely different meanings as short words).

Correct:	*Incorrect:*
in. [inch or inches]	in
no. [number]	no
lb [pound]	lb.
ft [foot or feet]	ft.
yd [yard or yards]	yd.
doz [dozen]	doz.

Abbreviations of phrases usually include a period after each letter.

Incorrect:

am.	pm.	eg.
am	pm	eg

Correct:

a.m.	p.m.	e.g.

Abbreviations of single words include one period only. Do not use two periods when an abbreviation comes at the end of a sentence.

Incorrect:
   I work as a receptionist for SampleCo, Inc..

Correct:
   I work as a receptionist for SampleCo, Inc.

3. Use the same abbreviation for singular and plural units of measurement.

When abbreviating a unit of measurement, use the same abbreviation for singular and plural.

1 cm	3 cm
1 ft	6 ft
1 gal	9 gal
1 yd	4 yd

4. For other plural abbreviations, add the letter *s* and place the period at the end.

Singular	*Plural*
mgr.	mgrs.
dept.	depts.
acct.	accts.

5. Spell out unfamiliar abbreviations the first time you use them.

When using an abbreviation not readily identified by your reader, clarify by using the full term at the first usage only. Use parentheses around the full word.

Example:

> From now on, the BRC (budget review committee) will
> meet every other Wednesday. Members of the BRC
> should notify their supervisors of this commitment at
> least one day prior to scheduled BRC meeting dates.

Some abbreviated names that contain more than one word
can be expressed by using capital letters in place of periods.

Acceptable formats:

> Rev.com.   RevCom   Revcom.

Such alternative usage is normal within an organization, where
such abbreviations become commonly recognized. When communicating to the outside, spelling out the name of an internal
group is a preferable practice.

Example:

> The Budget Review Committee of Greatco, Inc., meets
> every other Wednesday. The committee is responsible
> for ensuring that new policies and procedures meet
> management's objectives.

6.   Abbreviate titles only when they precede a name.

Titles should be abbreviated only when they precede an individual's name.

Incorrect:

> Our technical division is headed by a Dr.
> The speaker at today's luncheon is a prof. from the
> university.

Correct:

> Dr. Adams is vice president of our technical division.
> Prof. Johnson will speak at noon today.

Most abbreviations are not to be used as the first word in
a sentence. Titles are an exception; when titles are not spelled

out in common usage, such as *Mr.* and *Ms.,* they can be used to start a sentence.

Incorrect:

> Dept. supervisors will meet this morning.
> Mister Hansen reports to Ms. Green.

Correct:

> Department supervisors will meet this morning.
> Ms. Green is vice president of the finance division.

7. Observe punctuation rules.

When abbreviating a word before a comma or semicolon, remember to precede the punctuation mark with a period.

Incorrect:

> At GreatCo, Inc, employees receive good benefits.
> He was hired by GreatCo, Inc; it was the job he had long
>   been waiting for.

Correct:

> At GreatCo, Inc., employees receive good benefits.
> He was hired by GreatCo, Inc.; it was the job he had
>   long been waiting for.

An interrogatory sentence ending with an abbreviation should include a period followed by the question mark.

Incorrect:

> Is this GreatCo, Inc?

Correct:

> Is this GreatCo, Inc.?

See also: ACRONYMS; PUNCTUATION; TITLES

*   *   *

ACRONYMS

Acronyms are abbreviated names of longer multiword organizations or technologies. They are usually formed by taking the first letter from each word of a multiword combination in such a way that the abbreviation can be pronounced as a word.

1. Follow the rules of capitalization.

The letters of the acronym are usually capitalized when the first letters of the corresponding words are capitalized when spelled out. Some acronyms that describe technologies eventually come into such common use that they are lowercased, however.

> *Examples:*
> NASDAQ (National Association of Securities Dealers
>   Automated Quotations)
> System Plan Expenditure Numerical Database (SPEND)
> radar (*radio detecting and ranging*)

Some acronyms are constructed from syllables rather than from the letters of corresponding words or from a combination of syllables and letters.

> *Examples:*
> BUZOFF (Business Office Functions)
> AUTOCAP (Automatic Consumer Action Program)

Some acronyms are capitalized even though their corresponding words are not, and some commonly used acronyms are never capitalized. The rule to follow is that of convention; common usage dictates proper form, even though the result is inconsistent. Consult a dictionary for specific acronyms.

Examples:
> CAD (computer-aided design)
> cal (computer-aided learning)

2. Introduce unfamiliar acronyms to your reader.

When using an acronym in text for the first time, spell it out in full for the reader's benefit.

Examples:
> We intend to incorporate the System Tabulation and Evaluation Accounting Ledger (STEAL) as our primary financial control mechanism.

In order to introduce a new acronym, the full name can be spelled out, followed by the acronym, the first time it is used. The acronym can be placed within text, in quotation marks, or in parentheses.

Examples:
> Our project leader is a member of the Professional Association of Consulting Engineers, also known as PACE.
> The system is called the Automatic Tabulating, Listing, and Sorting System, or "ATLAS."
> Complaints should be directed to the Business Efficiency and Expediting Function (BEEF) office.

See also: Abbreviations

* * *

ACTIVE AND PASSIVE VOICE

Use of the active voice is preferable in most writing because it instantly identifies the action with the person who is performing that action. It creates strong, lively writing. In comparison, a passive voice form is less clear because it does not identify the doer of the action until much later in the sentence, and it sometimes avoids identifying the doer at all. Nevertheless, passive voice is sometimes useful to create variety within a paragraph, when you deliberately want to draw attention to the action rather than to who did it, or for emphasis.

1.   Learn the differences between active and passive.

The following examples demonstrate the differences in clarity between active and passive voice:

Active voice:
> My department prepared the report.
> I recommend that we perform a study.
> The division earned a profit last year.
> I will start working on that task next week.

Passive voice:
> The report was prepared by my department.
> The report was prepared.
> It is my recommendation that a study be performed.
> A profit was earned last year by the division.

2.   Be aware of your writing habits and traps.

Be aware of writing habits to avoid the trap of using passive voice when active voice is a better way of expressing yourself. Remember these rules of thumb:

- Avoid beginning sentences with the object rather than with the subject, or actor. "My department" is the actor that prepared "the report," the object. Place the actor before the noun and the object after the noun.
- Avoid indirect nouns, often represented at the beginning of a sentence with the words "it is." Your writing will improve vastly by simply avoiding this phrase. (See also *False Subjects*.) You may use indirect pronouns (*I*, *we*, or *me*, for example) in business writing and avoid the awkward sentence structure common to excessive passive voice sentences.
- Edit your writing by replacing passive voice sentences with the active voice. This change will clarify your statements by eliminating unnecessary and awkward construction.

3. Use passive voice when called for.

Passive voice is preferred in three instances:

1. When you do not know the identity of the subject.

Examples:
    The report was not prepared because essential
    information was not provided in time.
    Our company picnic was delayed because of unexpected
    changes in the weather.

2. When you want to place greater emphasis on the receiver than on the subject. By arranging sentences according to active or passive voice, you determine where emphasis is placed.

Examples:
    Complete documentation of procedures is required by our
    internal auditing department.
    Shanelle was hired by a major law firm.

3. To effect a better transition between thoughts.

Passive voice:
    The upcoming management seminar was planned to

include a forum for discussion of unnecessary
committees in business. A panel presentation for that
purpose is scheduled.

Without expressing the first sentence in the passive voice,
the transition would not have been as smooth.

Active voice:

Managers can discuss excessive use of committees in the
forum of the upcoming management seminar. A panel
presentation for that purpose is scheduled.

4. Change verbs to eliminate passive voice.

Replacing one verb with another or eliminating entire phrases
can clarify your writing while removing both passive voice and
unclear expression of ideas.

Before editing:

Accounting processes may be thought of as a means for
achieving balance control.

After editing:

Accounting processes achieve balance control.

See also: False subjects

*   *   *

Adjectives: *See* **Parts of Speech**

Adverbs: *See* **Parts of Speech**

AGREEMENT

Agreement, a basic rule of English grammar, states that singular-subject nouns must be accompanied by singular verbs and plural-subject nouns must be accompanied by plural verbs.

1. Connect singular nouns to singular verbs and plural subject nouns to plural verbs.

Singular-subject nouns are always connected to verbs that are also singular.

> *Examples:*
> The office is located downtown.
> The manager arrives today.

Plural-subject nouns are always connected to verbs that are also plural.

> *Examples:*
> The buildings are located downtown.
> The managers arrive today.

Avoid the common mistake of having the verb agree with its complement, not its subject.

> *Correct:*
> The topic of concern to management was expenditures
>   during the last quarter.

In this example, the subject *(topic)* and the verb *(was)* are in agreement. A common error is to have the verb agree with the complement *(expenditures)*.

Incorrect:

> The topic of concern to management were expenditures during the last quarter.

2. Connect compound subject nouns to compound verbs.

When a sentence contains more than one subject, the verb should be plural as well.

Incorrect:

> Supervisor and employee is required to follow this rule.

Correct:

> Supervisor and employee are required to follow this rule.

Subject nouns connected by joiners, as in the examples above, are usually accompanied by plural verbs. There is an exception: when the two subjects are in fact a single noun or when a single entity is made up of many parts.

Examples:

> Smith and Jones is our accounting firm
> Our best friend and worst enemy is the vocal customer.
> The company is responsible for its image.

Certain modifiers demand plural nouns. These include the words *both, few, several,* and *many.*

Examples:

> Few employees are working overtime.
> Many suppliers were planning price increases.

Some modifiers can confuse the selection of singular or plural verbs. The subject, however, dictates agreement.

Examples:

> All of the work is complete.
> All of the employees are in the office.

In the first example, *work* is a singular subject, so the verb, *is,* is singular as well. In the second example, *employees* is a plural subject, so the verb, *are,* is plural as well. The same rules apply to modifiers such as *any, more, most, none,* and *some.*

3. Use singular or plural verbs for collective nouns based on context.

Some nouns identify groups of individuals but are treated as singular subjects—for example, include *committee, group, public, government,* and *audience.* The verb used with these subjects depends on the context:

a. A singular verb is used when the subject refers to the group singularly.

Example:
> The committee is meeting in room 305.

b. A plural verb is substituted when reference is clearly to the individual members of the group.

Note, however, that as a question of form, this is an awkward style to employ.

Example:
> The committee are working through their agenda.

c. Subjects representing measurement or value are expressed in singular form when presented as one unit.

Examples:
> Four thousand dollars is too high a variance.
> Three months is enough time to complete a report.

d.   Special treatment is allowed in conventional use for certain words.

These include *data* and *number. Data* is a plural word whose singular form, *datum,* is rarely used. Increasingly, using *data* interchangeably is becoming common use and practice. Technically, however, only the plural form is correct.

Correct:
>   The data [plural] are compiled and available.

Incorrect but common:
>   The data [plural subject] is [singular verb] in my office.

The word *number* may be used in either singular or plural form, depending on the intent of the writer. Generally, if *number* is preceded by *the,* it is singular, and if preceded by *a,* it is plural.

Examples:
>   The number of employees [singular] is growing.
>   A number of employees [plural] are coming.

e.   Words ending in *-ics* are singular if referring to a science or body of information and plural if referring to action or a quality.

Examples:
>   Economics [singular] is the study of money.
>   The market tactics [plural] depend on the market.

4.   Avoid awkward phrases.

When subjects are connected with phrases such as *together with, as well as,* and *in addition to,* the subjects are treated as singular and should be coupled with singular verbs. This construction is often awkward, though, and should be avoided in the interest of clarity of expression.

Examples:

> Top management, together with each department, wants
> to work to improve profitability.
> The western division, as well as the central division, has
> effectively controlled costs.
> Proper procedures, in addition to controls, ensures lower
> budget variances.

Use of the phrase *one of those who* requires a plural verb. However, this is an awkward form of expression and should be replaced by a clearer, more concise alternative.

Examples:

> I am one of those who believe [plural] managers should
> become involved only if a problem emerges.
> I believe managers should become involved only if a
> problem emerges. [clearer alternative]

Some qualifying words require singular verbs when they are used in front of plural subjects—for example, *part, portion, series,* and *type.* Avoid using these phrases to eliminate awkward sentences.

Correct but awkward:

> Part of the activities in our department is [singular] the
> control of costs and expenses.

Clearer:

> Control of costs and expenses is one of the activities in
> our department.

5.   Do not be confused when a phrase intervenes between subject and verb.

When a phrase with a plural noun is inserted between a singular subject and the verb, the verb is singular.

Example:

A marketing plan [singular], including advertising budget or promotional efforts [plural], has [singular] been our most profitable way of moving products to market.

See also: SINGULAR AND PLURAL

*   *   *

ALPHABETIZING

There are two primary methods for alphabetizing: letter by letter and word by word. Use either one but only one; that is, make a decision and apply it consistently to avoid chronic problems in the filing system.

Under the letter-by-letter method, strict alphabetizing is applied regardless of where word breaks occur and regardless of spaces, commas, or periods. In the word-by-word method, a break occurs at the end of each word in a title or multiword name. Each unique word is completed before proceeding to the next.

Letter-by-Letter Method	*Word-by-Word Method*
Man, Barbara	Man, Barbara
Mane, J.	Man, M.J.
Manis, R.	Man, Steven
Man, M.J.	Mane, J.
Man, Steven	Manis, R.

1. Arrange names of people by last, first, and middle.

a. For proper names of individuals, alphabetize in the order of last name, first name, and middle initial.

Arrange all identical last names, followed by alphabetized first names, and third by middle initial.

Examples:
    Adams, Andrew A.
    Adams, Andrew B.
    Adams, Betty R.
    Adams, Charles L.
    Adams, Charles M.

b. Initials precede full names.

Examples:
    Adams, A.
    Adams, Andrew

c. Names beginning with *Mc* and *Mac* should be filed in strictly alphabetical order, regardless of capitalization or spacing within the name.

Examples:
    Mabley
    Mackinley
    MacTavish
    Mason
    McDonald

d. Prefixes should be treated as part of the name, regardless of capitalization or spacing.

Examples:
    de la Guardia
    Des Norte
    van der Hope
    von Schmidt

e. Alphabetize *St.* as though spelled out *Saint.*

f. File by name even when professional designations are Included.

Use designations only as a last default for filing otherwise identical names.

Name	File as:
Dr. Hal Adams	Adams, Hal, Dr.

g.   Alphabetize abbreviated names as though spelled out in full.

Name	File as:
Jones, Wm.	Jones, William
Smith, Chas.	Smith, Charles
Thomas, Bill	Thomas, William

h.   File nicknames in strict alphabetical order when the individual is known by that name. Cross-reference to legal names when known.

Name	File as:
Big Willy	Big Willy
Jones, William	*see* Big Willy
Illinois Al	Illinois Al
Jones, Al	*see* Illinois Al

2.   Name locations by unique name rather than designation.

a.   Alphabetize place names by the unique name, not by the type of place.

However, when the full name is the name of a city, file by the first word.

Name	File as:
Lake Tahoe [lake]	Tahoe, Lake
Lake Tahoe [city]	Lake Tahoe
Mount Adams [mountain]	Adams, Mount
Mount Adams [city]	Mount Adams

b.   File non-English article names (*de, el, la,* etc.) by article, as part of the full name.

Name	File as:
El Dorado	El Dorado
Los Angeles	Los Angeles

3. Name organizations by first name.

a. File organization names by the first word of the organization's name.

Name	File as:
Union Carbide	Union Carbide
Standard Oil	Standard Oil
The Smith Co.	Smith Co.

b. When the organization name is also a personal name, follow rule *a*.

Cross-reference the individual name.

Name	File as:
William Jones Corp.	William Jones Corp.
Jones, William, Corp.	*see* William Jones Corp.

c. Treat corporate names according to rules 3*a* and 3*b*, even when titles are used as part of the name.

Examples	File under:
Sly Guy Pizza	S
Captain Bob Parker	C
Miss Fashion	M
Happy Time	H

d. Disregard articles, conjunctions, prepositions, and punctuation in organizational names unless they are integral parts of the name.

Examples	File under:
The Anderson Co.	A
In the Know, Inc.	I
Oh Vermont	O

e. File abbreviated organizational names at the beginning of the letter category when companies are commonly known by those names.

Cross-reference the full name.

Name	File as:
IBM	IBM
International Business Machines	*see* IBM
MMM	MMM
Minnesota Mining and Manufacturing	*see* MMM

f. Some organizational names are derived from acronyms or purposely misspelled words.

Alphabetize exactly as spelled, ignoring spacing, capitalization, and punctuation.

Examples:
BusConsult
Business Consultants, Inc.
Buy-Chek
Buy-N-Sav
Buz Net

4. Alphabetize numbers as though they were spelled out.

Numbers should be alphabetized as though spelled out, whether expressed in alpha or numeric form.

Number	File as:
81	eighty-one
eight hundred	eight hundred
501	five hundred and one
1,000	one thousand
seven hundred	seven hundred
701	seven hundred and one
22	twenty-two
2	two

5. Cross-reference when placement is uncertain.

Provide file cross-references in the following circumstances:

- You are uncertain of the correct file placement.
- More than one version of the same name exists—an acronym, nickname, or alternative spelling.
- The organizational name is the same as the name of an individual.
- An exceptionally large file section is placed outside the normal filing sequence. For example, an insurance company may have a large section filed as "Claims." Under the "C" section in the main file, cross-reference to the location of "Claims" files.

6. Alphabetize consistently.

Be consistent with alphabetizing methods. Select your method for filing based on the volume, scope, and purpose of the files. Most business files should be arranged under the word-by-word method. The organization's filing policies should be described and summarized as a written procedure that all employees with access to the files can refer to. Periodic file audits can check for consistency of method.

*   *   *

Apostrophe: *SEE* **PUNCTUATION**

APPENDIXES

Appendixes are materials incidental to the main text in reports and other documents. By including appendixes, business writers can keep reports short and clear, with major points easily found in the main body of the report. Supplying the supporting data—statistics, lists, studies, tables, and so forth—in one or more appendixes can help the reader verify information of interest, without cluttering the report.

1. Use appendixes to keep the main report brief.

Short, easy-to-read reports get more attention from busy executives than longer, less organized ones. Emphasize the most important information in a one-page report summary, and break down the rest of the report in major sections. When additional but incidental information is referred to, create an appendix for it. Remember, however, that the shorter the report, the more effective it is. Do not include unnecessary information, even in an appendix.

2. Cross-reference materials accurately and thoroughly.

When a report refers to information supported by an appendix, include a cross-reference to the appendix, citing its number or title. Number appendix information separately from the body of the report. For example, begin numbering appendix A with page A-1; appendix B begins with page B-1.

3. Refer to appendixes in the document.

The most common application for use of appendixes is the business report, although other documents may require appendixes as well. An interoffice memorandum, for example, may refer to a lengthy study or other, longer documents. Include the referred-to-document only when necessary, and refer to it as an appendix to the memo. Alternatively, refer to the document in your memo, noting that the longer document is also available for review.

See also: REPORTS

*   *   *

Boldface: *SEE* HIGHLIGHTING IN TEXT

Brackets: *SEE* PARENTHESES AND BRACKETS

BUDGETS AND FORECASTS

The formats selected for written budget and forecast documents determine how well they are comprehended. The usefulness of these documents may be determined by how well they are presented.

1.   Set up explanatory narrative sections.

Budgets are primarily numbers: estimates of the financial future and explanations showing how those estimates were developed. Readers cannot comprehend numbers alone and need additional narrative summaries and explanations. Each summary should represent the major departments or divisions making up the entire budget. If you prepare the budget for only one department or section, you will need only one summary section. The section should contain as few numbers as possible and is most effective when limited to the following information:

- A brief description of the department or section, its work and purpose, and how it works with other sections of the organization.

- Methods employed in developing the budget, including basic assumptions concerning the financial direction anticipated during the budgetary period. Also describe policies or goals imposed on the section by management to the extent that those policies have affected the budget.
- Major departures from budgeting assumptions used in previous periods, including a short explanation of the previous year's budget versus actual results. When appropriate, include methods employed to reduce the likelihood of errors in the current budget.

2. Provide clear, concise cross-references.

The budget is a complex document with many numbers. Help the reader by providing consistent and concise cross-references between sections of the report. Be especially thorough in documenting the budget summary to supporting documents. Organize the budget report with numbered pages, and use consistent titles for account categories.

3. Follow usual practice for organization.

Arrange the report in the following manner (Figure B-1):

1. *Table of Contents*
2. *Summary sections,* which present the overall budget plan in narrative form
3. *Budget summary,* showing the full budgetary period, preferably by month
4. *Supporting documents,* to explain the assumptions used to develop the budget

4. Break down assumptions by source or type so that variations can later be identified in the same groupings.

For example, in the expense classification Advertising, major segments should include newspaper ad, radio, printed material, and other related classifications.

Figure B-1.   Recommended Way to Organize a Budget Report

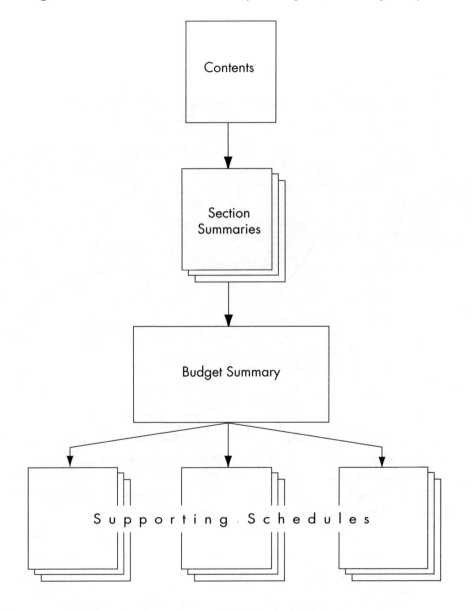

Each of these groupings should be budgeted separately on the assumption worksheet, and the total used for the category's budget. Later, actual expenses can be compared in the same classifications of budget.

In the case of income forecasts, include an adequate explanation of the assumptions used to develop each source of revenue. Attempt to tie revenue projections in your forecast to sources that can be monitored and identified.

5.   Design the budget report with monitoring in mind.

Preparing the budget report is only the first step in the budgeting process. A properly used budget serves as the document against which each month's actual outcome is measured. The supporting document section of the budget should be organized and designed so that assumptions can be tracked and variances explained completely.

See also: REPORTS; SAMPLE FORMS SECTION

*   *   *

CAPITALIZATION

A word is said to be capitalized when its first letter is capitalized. Commonly, *capitalized* does not imply that letters beyond the first letter are also expressed in capital letters. When a word is described as "all caps," every letter is capitalized. The abbreviation u.c. means "uppercase," or capitalize. The abbreviation l.c. means "lowercase."

1.   Capitalize the first letter in a proper noun but not in a common noun.

Proper nouns are the names of people, places, and organizations. Whenever these nouns are used, the first letter in the word is capitalized. A generalized reference—a common noun—is not capitalized.

Category	Proper Nouns	Common Nouns
Peoples' names and titles	Mary Adams	the woman
	Robert Brown	the man
	Dr. Anderson	the doctor
	President Connors	the president
Place names	New York	downtown
	London	the capital
	Lake Winston	a lake
	Mount Everest	the mountain
Organizations	American Pin Co.	the company
	University of Ohio	college
	Elks Club	the club
Brand names	Pepsi-Cola	a cola
	Big Mac	a burger
Days, months, and holidays	Wednesday	today
	September	last month
	Memorial Day	a holiday
Historical references	World War II	the war
	Battle of the Bulge	the battle
Titles of religions and deities	Catholic church	church
	God	the gods
Titles of publications	*The Quest*	a book
	The New York Times	a paper

2. Capitalize the first word of a sentence.

The first word of every sentence is capitalized. In an outline, the first letter of each subsection is capitalized. A quotation within a sentence begins with a capital letter unless the quotation begins in the middle of a sentence.

Examples:

The procedures manual states, "Reports will be due by the fifth day of each month."

The procedures manual states that reports "will be due by the fifth day of the month."

3. Capitalize titles of books, magazines, and other published materials.

Titles of books, magazines, and organizations should be capitalized. However, articles *(a, an, the)*, coordinating conjunctions *(and, for, nor, or)*, and prepositions under four letters are lowercased *unless* they are the first or last word.

> *Examples:*
> *New York Times Magazine* [newspaper]
> *Leadership Secrets of Attila the Hun* [article]
> *Of Human Bondage* [book]
> *"Muddling Through"* [article]
> International Business Machines [organization]

4. Follow the rules for special situations.

Special rules or style decisions have to be made when dealing with special situations.

a. Geographic regions:

Decide when to capitalize based on whether a specific region is meant (capitalized) or a general direction or area (do not capitalize).

Specific Region	*General Direction*
the East	moving east
the South	south of here
West Texas	western Texas

b. Heading words:

Capitalize headings unless they are articles.

> *Examples:*
> Audit-Proofed Data System
> State-of-the-Art Computerized Model

c. Sections of documents:

When sections are mentioned in text (appendix 1, figure 6, and volume II, for example) they should not be capitalized as a general rule. Nevertheless, they often are capitalized in order to emphasize them. Choose one method, and be consistent.

5. Use capitalization as a form of emphasis.

In some situations, you can use capitalization to emphasize isolated words you want the reader to pay attention to.

Examples:
The division reported a PROFIT this quarter.
Our goal is NOT to provide free services.

6. Avoid overusing capitalization.

Avoid overuse of capitals and all-caps in documents. Excessive use is distracting to the reader and does not add value to the message.

Examples:
The Division Reported A Profit This Quarter.
THE DIVISION REPORTED A PROFIT THIS QUARTER.

In both of these examples, capitals are used inappropriately and excessively.

See also: CAPTIONS; HEADINGS; HIGHLIGHTING IN TEXT

*   *   *

CAPTIONS

Captions are brief descriptive phrases or sentences accompanying charts, graphs, photographs, and other visual representations in reports.

1. Use descriptive captions to guide readers in interpreting visual information.

Captions may be titles only or full sentences. When using a full-sentence, descriptive caption, end it with a period. Use descriptive captions to emphasize the key information presented in a graph or other illustration.

Descriptive captions:
> The rate of profits has exceeded forecasts in every quarter.
> The per-employee expense declined after our new budgeting controls went into effect.

2. Use only brief title captions in technical reports and appendixes.

Some charts and graphs are self-explanatory and need only titles (but be sure to use a title). Use title captions as well when you do not want to editorialize beyond the presentation of data. In these cases, do not place a period or other punctuation at the end of the caption. Capitalize each important word in a title caption (do not capitalize conjunctions and prepositions with fewer than four letters).

Brief captions:
> Rate of Profits
> Per-Employee Expense

3. Place captions consistently.

Place title captions above or below graphics. Decide on placement, and be consistent throughout a single report. Always place full-sentence captions beneath the graphic.

4. Accompany captions with numbered references.

Graphics are effective ways to communicate information in reports quickly and effectively. The caption is especially useful when a report contains a large volume of financial information. Preface each caption with a reference number—Figure (or Table) 1, for example—so that the reader can quickly find the graphic mentioned in the text.

See also: CHARTS AND GRAPHS; HEADINGS

*   *   *

CHARTS AND GRAPHS

Most business reports concern numbers—data concerning finances, profits, production, marketing, and other numerical information—that is best understood when displayed graphically. As a result, charts and graphs are valuable business tools. Readers understand information better and retain more of it when it is presented visually than when it is presented verbally or in print.

1. Keep charts and graphs in scale.

The *scale* is the value representation used in the graphic—for example, dollars, units of production, or employees. One side of the graphic is used for the value and the other for a distinction, such as reporting periods (month, quarter, fiscal year), divisions, or companies.

The scale must be an accurate representation. For values, this means the baseline should be at zero. The graphic representation for information beginning above zero will appear inaccurate. The graphic should also be at such a scale that the size is reasonable for the report and easy to read. A square or a rectangle approximating a square is most practical in the majority of applications.

2.   Keep scales the same throughout a single report.

Select a scale based on consistency and use it for reporting similar data throughout the report. Otherwise, the relative value of similar information will be distorted. Dissimilar information invariably requires different scaling.

3.   Cross-reference charts and graphs to the text.

Graphics within the body of the report or appendixes should be carefully cross-referenced to the page number in the report or the proper section of a larger report. Narrative referring to charts and graphs should identify them by graphic number (e.g., "see Figure 1") and by location (e.g., "see below" or "see the next page").

4.   Provide brief captions to distinguish graphics.

Captions should tell the reader at a glance exactly what the graphic shows. Even complex graphics can usually be reduced to a few words. The caption makes a distinction between otherwise very similar graphs in the same report or on the same page.

A brief descriptive caption can be used to emphasize the most important point of the graphic. For example, a graph can be labeled, "Sales and Net Profits," telling the reader precisely what the graph reveals. Captions may be longer than a brief title when appropriate. In this example, a longer caption could read, "The rate of net profits has increased during a period of rising sales volume."

5. Strive for simplicity.

Graphics can show numerous results; however, an important rule of presentation is that simplicity is easier to convey and, from the reader's point of view, much easier to understand and retain. A single graph can be designed to show yearly results in comparative form, for several divisions, and broken down by different product lines; however, much important detail might be lost. It may be preferable to break out some comparisons in several similar graphs, and discuss each one briefly in text.

6. Select the best graphic to convey information.

No one graphic is suitable for every situation. In a lengthy report containing a great deal of complex financial information, variety in style of presentation is desirable. Too many similar charts and graphs confuses the reader; specialized charts and graphs invariably improve the overall impression.

a. Chart or table:

Use charts and tables within a narrative section to highlight financial information.

A table:

Sales by Division (in millions)

	Current Year	Prior Year
Durables	$1,244	$1,006
Parts	603	719
All other	154	89
Total	$2,001	$1,814

Figure C-1. Line Graph. The dashed and solid lines show projected and actual values.

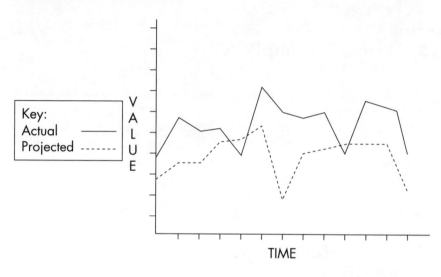

b. Line graph:

One of the most popular types of visual aids, the line graph is most useful for showing two or more comparative values over a specific period of time—for example, actual versus budget in a yearly or quarterly summary; sales compared to forecasts, or sales in two or more periods over a year; and other comparisons of financial information over a time line. In the typical line graph shown in Figure C-1, the value is reflected from top to bottom (in the vertical axis), often meaning dollars or units of production; time is shown from left to right (horizontal axis). This graphic is most commonly used for reporting business results and is the most compatible with accepted reporting methods, since dollar results are reported over a period of time in financial reports.

c. Bar graph:

This type of graph is best used for showing comparative information in total or for one moment in time (as opposed to a dynamic

Figure C-2. Vertical Bar Graph

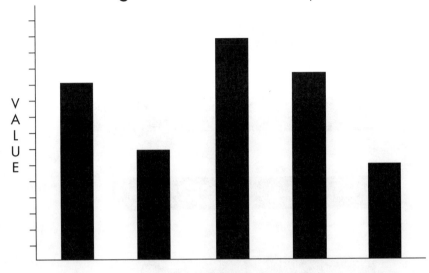

COMPARISON

report in monthly, quarterly, or annual periods). Two types can be used. The vertical bar graph, shown in Figure C-2, is useful for demonstrating levels of financial information for a limited number of comparisons (departments, divisions, or areas, for example). Value (such as dollars) is shown from top to bottom, and the comparative distinction is listed in the bars from left to right. A typical example would be total sales volume (value) by division (comparison).

The same information may be presented in the horizontal bar graph, which is useful when a larger number of factors are being compared. Because of its horizontal shape, a longer graph can be represented without exceeding the width limits of a standard-sized page. In Figure C-3, the value is shown from left to right, and the comparison bars are shown from top to bottom. When the value results are shown for several different comparisons, the bars themselves can be coded, as in Figure C-4. Sales results are shown for four different divisions in the same year, and each bar has a different color or shading.

Figure C-3. Horizontal Bar Graph

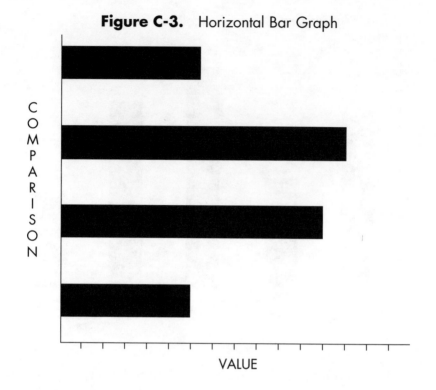

d. Pie chart:

This chart is also used to report results for one block of time. The example in Figure C-5 breaks down expenses for one year, by percentage. While a line graph might show the relative dollar values of each expense category by month, the pie chart shows a visual breakdown of the entire year. Simply reporting percentages does not give the same impact. The pie chart makes the information visual, enabling the reader to understand how much of the total is spent on each broad classification of expense.

Figure C-6 shows how such a pie chart is constructed. The percentages shown in Figure C-5 are converted by multiplying each by 360 (degrees).

Figure C-4. Bar Graph with Coded Bars

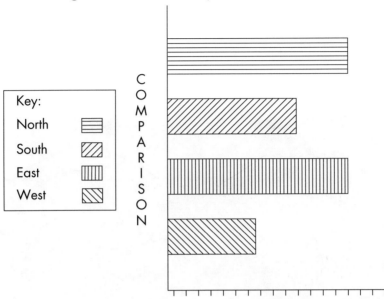

Figure C-5. Pie Chart

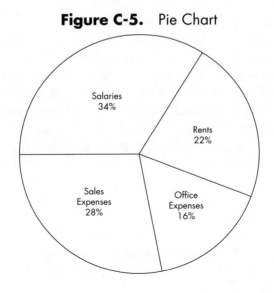

Figure C-6.   How a Pie Chart Is Constructed

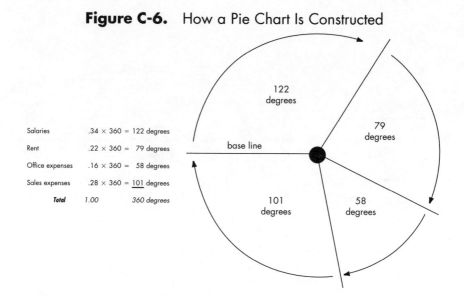

Salaries	.34 × 360 =	122 degrees
Rent	.22 × 360 =	79 degrees
Office expenses	.16 × 360 =	58 degrees
Sales expenses	.28 × 360 =	101 degrees
Total	1.00	360 degrees

7. Use charts and graphs for scheduling and planning control.

Some specialized charts and graphs are suited for the control of planning and scheduling of projects. Figure C-7 shows one form of a Gantt chart; it uses two variations of rectangular boxes. Functions are listed on the left from top to bottom; time is reflected from left to right. The unfilled rectangular boxes indicate planned time required for each task, and the filled boxes are used for actual time. Because this chart allows you to see at a glance how planning and implementation are working, this technique is especially useful for complex projects requiring numerous functions. It helps you to anticipate time delays well in advance since many functions overlap in time.

An alternative method involves using blank or filled-in triangles to reflect the same information. In Figure C-8, a triangle pointing upward indicates the starting point; a triangle pointing downward is the planned or actual completion date. The advantage of this type of Gantt chart is that the planned and actual scheduling can all be placed on a single line.

Figure C-7. Gantt Chart

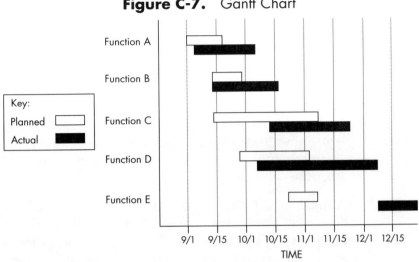

This Gantt chart uses a bar format. In this example, Function E could not begin until Function D was completed, so the project was late.

Figure C-8. Alternative Gantt Chart Using Lines With Triangles Instead of Bars

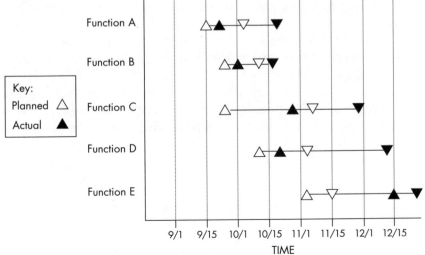

8. Use charts and graphs to improve presentations.

When making presentations at meetings, use charts and graphs to convey information clearly and effectively. Most people retain visual information more completely than they do written or verbal information.

A particularly useful meeting tool is the transparency: a chart, graph, or other information printed on a transparent film and shown through an overhead projector. Following are some guidelines for transparencies:

- *Keep it simple.* The more complex that diagrams, drawings, and other visual aids are, the less effective they are. Transparencies should be extremely easy to grasp, and should be used to support a point you are trying to make. Think of the transparency as a tool to improve the relating of information, never as an excuse for a complete, clear explanation.
- *Keep words to a minimum.* Having too much to read on what is supposed to be a visual aid defeats the purpose. The fewer words, the better. Never use a transparency that consists only of words.
- *Keep all transparencies at the same scale.* If you are conveying similar types of information through the use of overhead transparencies, keep the scale the same whenever possible. If you are forced to alter the scale because of sizing and presentation, be sure to point out to your audience that what they are viewing is not comparable to other transparencies.
- *Two to three colors are enough.* With modern technology, the production of multicolor transparencies is simple. Nevertheless, avoid overly colorful and elaborate graphics, which can be confusing or take too much time to figure out. Simplicity is still the best way to convey information so that your audience's interest remains high.

See also: CAPTIONS; PHOTOGRAPHS; PROPOSALS; REPORTS

*   *   *

CITATIONS

Some business reports and other correspondence refer to other works. In such cases, crediting the source is often necessary. This is the case when:

- The source is statistical, and citing it adds credibility to the report.
- A quotation or conclusion makes a point for the report and the citation is necessary by way of verifying information.
- The information presented was developed by someone else or comes from a separate source, published or unpublished.

1. Cite your sources in a bibliography.

The bibliography is a section at the end of reports, books, or memos that lists the sources used as reference material. It may contain a number of sources that are not specifically cited within the document, or specific references may be made by way of footnotes to the sources.

a. Book citations:

The format for citation varies considerably, depending on the purpose of the document and the publishing medium; however, some general rules should be followed for all citations from books. Entries are organized in alphabetical order by author's last name. Each entry contains the title, the city of publication, the publisher, and the year of publication.

1. Author: When two authors are credited, their names are listed in the same order in which they appear on the title page. When more than three authors are included, the first author's name is listed, followed by the abbreviation "et al." When an editor is credited for collections of essays in book form, the editor's name is followed with the abbreviation, "Ed."

2. Title: The title of the book follows, and is placed in italics, ending with a period. If the title itself includes sentence endings other than a period (such as exclamation or question marks), those are used in place of the period.

3. Place of publication: The city in which the book was published is listed next. If the city is well known (such as New York or Boston), no state is included. If the city of publication is obscure, the city name should be followed by a comma and the state abbreviation. The city of publication segment is ended with a colon.

4. Publisher: Next comes the publisher's name. If the publisher's name includes ending terms like "and Company" or "Inc.," such additions are excluded.

5. Date: The entry ends with the date, followed by a period.

Citations for books:

Evans, Wendy, et al. *Border Crossings.* Scarborough, Ont.: Prentice-Hall Canada, 1992.
Fischer, Frank, and Sirianni, Carmen, eds. *Critical Studies in Organization and Bureaucracy.* Philadelphia: Temple University Press, 1984.
Makridakis, Spyros, and Wheelwright, Steven C. *Forecasting Methods for Management.* New York: Wiley, 1989.
Thomsett, Michael C. *The Little Black Book of Business Math.* New York: AMACOM, 1988.

In these examples, note that entries are arranged alphabetically by the first-appearing last name. The first example is of a book with three authors; only the first is listed by name. Whenever "et al." or another author is listed, a comma must both follow and precede the first author's name. This entry also has a city of publication not widely known, so the province is included as well. The second entry involves editors rather than authors. The city is given without state reference because it is a well-known city. The third entry includes two authors and a well-known city. Note also that the publisher's full name is "John Wiley & Sons." However, only the essential name of the company is included in the citation. The fourth and final example involves one author of a book published in a prominent city, so the state is not listed.

When the book is not authored by an individual, list the organization's name as author.

Citation for a book authored by an organization:
Consumer Guide. *Money-Saving Toll-Free Phone Book.* New York: Beekman House, 1983.

b. Magazine, periodical, and newspaper citations:

The format for citing articles in newspapers and magazines is similar to that of books, as are the rules for method of citation. The article's title or headline is included, as well as the main publication. In addition, the publication volume number, month and page numbers are included. For a newspaper or other periodical published other than monthly, the precise date is given.

Magazine and periodical citations:
Lemann, Nicholas. "The Structure of Success in America." *Atlantic Monthly 51* (August 1995):41–60.
Rindlaub, John. "Steering to Prosperity." *Washington CEO* (July 1995):49.
Kelly, Tom. "Mortgages Keep Changing, So Ask Plenty of Questions." *The Seattle Times* (March 19, 1995):G-1.

c. Unpublished works:

Follow the same format as for published works to the degree possible (author, title, source, year).

Citations of unpublished works:

Brown, Martha. "Solving the Automated Transition Problem." Speech presented at Ames Corp. seminar, February 24, 1996.

Green, J. Letter to the author. May 17, 1995.

2. Place book citations properly.

Within the body of the report or book, specific reference to sources is given in one of several ways.

a. Within the narrative itself:

The author's last name and the publication date are given. The complete citation is given in the bibliography.

Citation in the narrative:

A recent survey (Smith, 1996) reveals that the majority of such cases are not profitable.

b. Footnotes:

An asterisk or numbered reference in the text is accompanied by a note at the bottom of the page, in one of two ways: (1) the author and year alone are given, as in [a] above; or the full author and book title are given in the first such reference, with the author's last name and a shortened title only in subsequent references.

c. Endnotes:

These notations follow the same rule as footnotes. However, notes are presented collectively (1) at the end of a section or chapter or (2) all together at the end of the report.

See also: FOOTNOTES; QUOTATIONS

*   *   *

CLICHÉS

A cliché is a form of expression familiar to people that identifies a range of sentiments.

1. Avoid cliché expressions.

Some writers fall into the habit of using clichés, hoping to convey an idea efficiently. Unfortunately, the use of clichés is distracting and reduces the effectiveness of writing.

A cliché:

We are in a "catch-22" situation.

A better choice:

Either way, we will probably lose.

A cliché:

It's six of one, a half dozen of the other.

A better choice:

It doesn't make any difference.

Cliché expressions common to business situations:

A-OK	bird in the hand
add insult to injury	bite the bullet
all and sundry	bottom line
back to the drawing board	brain trust
back to the salt mine	business as usual
be that as it may	cast pearls before swine
beat a dead horse	catch as catch can
beat around the bush	child's play
bed of roses	clear the air
behind the eight-ball	cold feet
beside the point	conspiracy of silence

cream of the crop
cut and dried
damn with faint praise
dog eat dog
dot the i's and cross the t's
draw a blank
dutch treat
dyed in the wool
easy pickings
eleventh hour
embarrassment of riches
enemy at the gate
explore every avenue
fact of the matter
fair and square
fair to middling
far and away
far cry
fat cat
feast or famine
feel the pinch
few and far between
fine-tooth comb
finger in every pie
first magnitude
fish out of water
fits and starts
fly in the face of
follow in the footsteps
for what it's worth
force to be reckoned with
fortunes of war
from A to Z
from bad to worse
full head of steam
get a handle on it
get a leg up on
get in on the ground floor
get to the bottom of it
give pause
go against the grain
go for broke

go hat in hand
go it alone
grin and bear it
grist for the mill
half the battle
hand in glove
hand over fist
handwriting on the wall
hard and fast
head in the clouds
heads will roll
hem and haw
high and dry
high-water mark
hit or miss
hit pay dirt
hit the nail on the head
hog the limelight
hoist by his own petard
hold at bay
hold the fort
hold your own
hope against hope
huff and puff
if worse comes to worst
ill-gotten gains
in a nutshell
in a word
in hot water
in the bag
in the long run
ivory tower
jaundiced eye
keep the ball rolling
kid-glove treatment
know the ropes
knuckle under
last but not least
last legs
last resort
last straw
lay our cards on the table

leave no stone unturned
left hand doesn't know
   what the right hand is
   doing
left in the lurch
left to your own devices
lesser of two evils
let sleeping dogs lie
let the chips fall where
   they may
let's face it
letter perfect
lion's share
long and the short of it
long shot
long suit
looking down his nose
lost cause
loud and clear
low man on the totem pole
make a virtue of necessity
make ends meet
make no bones about it
man of few words
mark my words
mind over matter
mine of information
moment of truth
moral victory
more or less
movers and shakers
naked truth
needless to say
nothing to write home
   about
off and running
on the ball
on the carpet
on the level
on the ropes
open secret
other things being equal

out of the woods
out on a limb
pack it in
part and parcel
pay the piper
pay through the nose
penny wise and pound
   foolish
pick and choose
pick his brain
play it by ear
play with fire
point of no return
pound of flesh
powers that be
pull it off
pull out all the stops
pull strings
pure and simple
push comes to shove
put on hold
put on the back burner
put your best foot forward
quick study
rack your brain
rat race
read the tea leaves
rings a bell
roll with the punches
rule of thumb
run of the mill
saving face
second to none
see it through
see red
see the light
sign of the times
sit tight
sitting pretty
six of one, half a dozen of
   the other
sixth sense

sky's the limit
smoke it out
snow job
so far, so good
sooner or later
spill the beans
steer clear of
straight from the shoulder
take it or leave it
take it with a grain of salt
taken to the cleaners
tell tales out of school
tempest in a teapot
then and there
there's the rub
throw caution to the winds
tighten your belt
time and again
tip of the iceberg
tit for tat
toe the line
too many irons in the fire
too much of a good thing
tough nut to crack

tower of strength
turn a deaf ear
turn back the clock
turning point
two sides to every question
unwritten law
up to snuff
uphill battle
vested interest
vicious circle
watchful eye
wave of the future
wearing two hats
well and good
when all is said and done
whys and wherefores
win hands down
wing it
wishful thinking
word to the wise
world of good
year in and year out
you get what you pay for

See also: JARGON

*　　*　　*

Colon: *SEE* PUNCTUATION

Comma: *SEE* PUNCTUATION

COMPOUND WORDS

A compound word is a term formed by two or more other words. It may be expressed as a single word *(workplace)*, a hyphenated word *(mind-set)*, or two words *(task force)*. Often there is an authoritative source for using the word, such as a dictionary, but for many words, especially adjective forms, you will have to apply rules.

1. Start by consulting a dictionary.

See whether there is an established style—single word, hyphenated, or two words—for a particular compound word. This is often the case for nouns.

2. Follow common usage.

Hyphenate a temporary compound word that is not in common usage or when custom does not dictate the creation of a single word. Many compound words that were originally hyphenated lose the hyphen as a result of common usage. The current trend is to use fewer hyphenated compounds and more single words.

Examples:
> The computer-literate group has a competitive advantage.
> A craze-for-profits mood does not always mean good
> news for the customer.

3. Hyphenate adjective forms before a noun but not after.

Adjective form before a noun:
> best-equipped department

Adjective form after a noun:
> department is best equipped

4. Be consistent in form.

Strive for consistency of form within a document. When you are uncertain whether a compound word should be hyphenated or kept separate, choose a form and use it consistently in the document.

5. Learn the rules of usage for hyphens.

a. Use hyphens when the compound word takes the form of an adjective.

Examples:

near-perfect marketing plan
slow-profits year

b. Do not hyphenate when the first half of the compound word ends in *-ly.*

Examples:

nearly perfect marketing plan
disappointingly slow year

c. Do not use a hyphen when the compound word is a verb.

Examples:

Be sure to follow up on the assignment.
Let's run through the presentation.

6. Close up words without hyphens when compounds are formed with prefixes.

Examples:

antedate	biweekly	cooperate
overflow	postscript	underreport

*   *   *

Conjunctions: *SEE* PARTS OF SPEECH

Dash: *SEE* PUNCTUATION

DECIMALS, FRACTIONS, AND PERCENTAGES

Business communication involves extensive use of numbers and numerical values. Clarity in documents depends on the ability of the writer to select the best method of explanation. Decimals, fractions, and percentages are different methods for expressing the same values:

Decimal	Fraction	Percentage
0.5	$\frac{1}{2}$	50%
0.75	$\frac{3}{4}$	75%
1.2	$1\frac{1}{5}$	120%

Decimals

The decimal point divides a value into whole and partial sides. Values to the left of the decimal point are whole numbers; values to the right are partial values (less than one). The number of digits to the right indicates the number of zeros following "1" in the lower half of an equivalent fraction:

Decimal	Fraction
0.333	$\frac{333}{1000}$
0.2	$\frac{2}{10}$
0.55	$\frac{55}{100}$

1. If the decimal value does not have any value to the left, insert a zero.

Examples:
0.25
0.77

2. Drop zeros to the far right of a decimal value.

Examples:
.25 (not .2500]
.75001 (not .750010]

3. When there are exceptionally long decimal values, separate them into groups of three.

Commas are never used within a decimal value.

Incorrect use:
78.356979493
78.356,979,493

Correct use:
78.356 979 493

4. Line up decimal values presented in a column.

Examples:
27.1
305.667
26
42.77732

5. In narratives, avoid beginning sentences with decimal values.

Incorrect use:
75.3 customers enter our store each day.

Correct use:
Each day 75.3 customers enter our store.

Fractions

Fractions, like decimals, are methods of expressing portions of a whole. A fraction contains a top and a bottom number. To convert fractions to decimals, divide the top number (the numerator) by the bottom number (the denominator).

Example:

$$3/4 = \frac{3}{4} = .75$$

1. Spell out fractions in narrative.

Fractions in narratives are usually spelled out and hyphenated.

Examples:
one-fifth
three-fourths

If the use of hyphenated fractions is awkward, convert to decimal or percentage form.

Examples of awkward hyphenation:
Fifteen-three hundredths = 5 percent *or* 0.05
Ten-eightieths = 12.5 percent *or* .125

2. Avoid using complex fractions.

Avoid using excessively long fractions. As a guideline, any fraction that is difficult to imagine should be converted to decimal form.

Example:
$^{23}/_{1000} = 0.234$

3. Do not spell out fractions when expressing units of measurement.

Use fractions in text when they are expressed with units of measurement. In these instances, do not spell out the fraction.

Examples:
4½ hours
3½ feet

Percentages

Percentages are alternative forms of expression for values, like decimals and fractions. A percentage is a portion of the whole. In business, percentages are commonly used to describe segmentation of overall values: profits, sales, employees, markets, and budgets. Just as common is the use of percentages to describe degrees of change (percentage of increase or decrease in financial value).

1. Use the proper format for communicating percentages.

In sentences, spell out the word *percent* rather than use the symbol.

Example:
Sales volume grew by 14 percent last year.

In tables and reports, use the percentage symbol rather than the word. When percentages appear in a column, only the first line and the total should be accompanied by the symbol.

Example:

Region	Amount	Percentage
West	$ 23,851	8%
East	107,900	37
North	42,830	15
South	118,347	40
	$292,928	100%

2. Know when to use percentage or decimal combinations.

When the percentage is less than 1 percent, express it in decimal form.

Example:
0.5 percent of employees [this is equal to one-half of 1 percent]

3. Strive for clarity in communication.

A percentage expression is often more effective than decimals or fractions. Use percentages to make the message clear.

Decimal expression:
Sales were 1.2 times greater.

Fraction expression:
Sales were 1 ⅕ times greater.

Percentage expression:
Sales were 120 percent greater.

*   *   *

DENOTATION AND CONNOTATION

The meaning of a word is its *denotation*, or what it denotes or refers to. A *concrete word* identifies a specific, tangible person, place, or thing (e.g., *typewriter, New York City, Bob*). A *relative word* describes qualities or degrees, or modifies another word (e.g., *red, high, low, hot, cold, impossible*). Finally, an *abstract word* refers to an idea or concept without specifying one type or example (e.g., *ability, intelligence, ambition, idea*).

The quality or suggestion of words is referred to as *connotation*. When the denotation of a word is understood, the next step is to understand the broad range of connotations that words carry. For example, the word *hot* may mean *spicy*. However, it can also refer to the weather, demand of a product with customers, one's appearance or clothing, or a fit of temper. Many words have a wide range of connotations. Even a fairly straightforward word or phrase may have connotations that are implied in the context of use, without being specified. Consider the following applications of the phrase *big business:*

> I want a career in big business.
> The environment has suffered because of the practices of big business.
> We're going into town today to conduct some big business.

The real meaning of words involves both denotation and connotation. The subtlety of style and expression depend on proper uses of phrases. Everyone has seen examples of writing that is factual, yet places a specific slant through connotation.

Example:

> The business interests of some out-of-town investors have led to development pressures in the area. There can be no doubt that these interests are guided by the profit motive. Because these investors do not live here, they are not as aware as we locals are of our heartfelt concerns.

This paragraph is loaded with connotation. There are no factual errors or lies within the statements themselves, yet the writer is clearly opposed to the "outsiders" and their motives.

Writers have to deal with numerous style decisions in everything they write, all in the effort to find the most suitable way to express their ideas. There is no one right word for every situation; many words may contain the right denotation yet not convey an idea as accurately or as precisely as another choice. The writer's skill and vocabulary determine how an idea is conveyed.

See also: STYLE AND TONE

* * *

DESKTOP PUBLISHING

Desktop publishing software enables businesses to develop professional-quality documents without the need for expensive and time-consuming outside services. Examples of business applications include reports that incorporate graphics and a variety of type styles; in-house newsletters, brochures, and pamphlets; procedures manuals, complete with graphic teaching aids; and the incorporation of important graphic and financial reporting with narratives. In the past, sophisticated design systems were expensive. Today, highly versatile systems are available for relatively little cost and can be learned along with a word processing system.

1. Design desktop publishing applications with the purpose in mind.

The application and use of desktop publishing should be determined by the purpose. A memo can be typed and delivered internally using a simple standard format. A marketing brochure, in comparison, has to make a different impact. The writing style, quality of paper and type, and graphics all add to the overall impression.

Desktop publishing systems offer a wide array of possible designs. That does not mean they all have to be (or should be) used. Simplicity and uniformity of design make a more professional impression than too many style and design changes.

2. Consider time and cost in advance.

Systems vary. Easy-to-use systems tend to be more expensive; less expensive systems tend to be less flexible and, perhaps, more difficult to master. Consider the time and cost in learning to use a new system, creating documents for the intended audience, and the benefit created by the use of a desktop publishing system. For internal uses only, excessive time and cost commitments for appearance only are not justified. In comparison, documents going outside the organization should be produced with great concern for the impression they create.

3. Select the typeface and size.

The design of a document encompasses a number of considerations, among them, columns, headings, the interjection of graphics, and variety of type size and typeface. *Typeface* is the style of letter. Some styles are more appropriate than others for professional documents. Follow these general guidelines:

- Stay with one style throughout a document for the most part. Use a second style only to emphasize key points or for headings in distinct sections.
- Avoid typefaces with excessive flourishes, shadings, and embellishments.
- For a professional-looking result, select typefaces with proportional spacing (laser fonts).
- Use italics, underlining, and boldface sparingly. Excessive use of these devices is distracting and negates the intended effect of drawing special attention to a limited number of words.

Figure D-1.   Font and Size Samples

8–point type
10–point type
12–point type
14–point type
16–point type

24–point type

36–point

proportional spacing
nonproportional spacing

lightface, **boldface,** *italic*

Palatino
Avant Garde
Times New Roman

- Limit the use of varying point sizes (the height of letters) within one document. Generally, two or three different point sizes are appropriate. The largest is reserved for titles; the smallest should be used for footnotes and captions.
- Stay within a comfortable range of point size for the main body of the text, and use that size throughout. The most common and comfortable are 10 point and 12 point. (See Figure D-1.)

*   *   *

Diacritical Marks: *SEE* **PUNCTUATION**

EDITING AND PROOFREADING

Editing is a process of review of written material to check for clarity, grammar, accuracy, and problems in expression considering the audience. Effective editing requires correction of problems so that the written message is clear and concise and conveys ideas well.

Proofreading is a process undertaken to ensure that a copy reproduces correctly the original material from which it was transcribed. A proofreader ensures that all words (and numbers) are correct and that all spelling is correct. Also to be checked are any corrections indicated from the original draft.

Editing

A careful, considerate, and insightful editor is at least as valuable to the finished product as a competent writer. The editor's function contributes importantly to the overall quality of communication.

1.   Understand the true meaning of the message.

A sensitive editor is responsible for determining the writer's true message. The meaning of a document can be unintentionally altered with careless editing.

> *Original text:*
> Managers responsible for filing such reports should be aware of the deadlines and of related fines imposed on the company for missing them.

> *Poorly edited text with distorted meaning:*
> Managers who file reports may also impose fines on the company for missing deadlines.

Correctly edited text:
> Managers filing reports should be aware of deadlines
> and understand that fines are imposed on the company
> if those deadlines are missed.

2.   Edit to simplify.

Good editing clarifies and simplifies. Avoid editing excessively
so that a message is made less clear. In many cases, removing
words is the best way to simplify a message.

Original text:
> Cognizant management personnel are advised to inform
> staff within their departments of the applicable holiday
> on Monday, May 28.

Editing that complicates the message:
> Those cognizant management personnel are hereby
> advised that it is imperative to advise employees within
> their departmental areas of the applicable holiday that
> occurs this Monday, May 28.

Editing that simplifies and clarifies:
> Managers are reminded to tell employees that this
> Monday, May 28, is a holiday.

3.   Respect the writer's style.

When editing someone else's work, respect that person's style
and method of expression, unless they are clearly inappropriate
for the audience. The editor's job is to fix, not to change, the
document. When the style is inappropriate to the degree that the
entire document has to be rewritten, the editor should provide
guidelines to the writer.

4.   Remember point of view and voice.

Business documents should contain the proper point of view and
voice. In formal reports, personal opinions and the first person
(*I, me, my*) are rarely used. Third-person voice is preferred.

First-person voice:

> I recommend this course of action.
> If it were up to me, I would reject that idea.
> My opinion is that we should take action.

Third-person voice:

> This course of action is recommended.
> That idea should be rejected.
> Taking action is the best course.

Figure E-1. Commonly Used Proofreading Marks

align horizontally	=	hyphen insert	=
align vertically	‖	italics	(ital)
asterisk insert	⋆	let stand	(stet)
apostrophe insert	⌄	letter insert	∧
boldface	(bf)	lower case	/
bracket insert	[/]	move section	↻
capitalize	≡	move down	⊔
center	] [	move up	⊓
close space	◯	move to the left	[
colon insert	:|	move to the right	]
comma insert	⌃	new paragraph	¶
dagger	⊕	parentheses insert	(/)
delete	ℯ	period insert	⊙
double dagger	⊕	quotation marks insert	⌄
double space	ds[	semicolon insert	;|
em dash	$\frac{1}{m}$	single space	ss[
en dash	$\frac{1}{n}$	space insert	# ∧
flush left	(fl)	spell out	(sp)
flush right	(fr)	transpose	∼

Proofreading

1. Proofread carefully and consistently.

2. Mark up the document to correct problems in spelling, grammar, or the sequence of words and phrases.

Proofreaders check spelling, grammar, and punctuation. Figure E-1 shows commonly used proofreading marks.

See also: ACTIVE AND PASSIVE VOICE; AGREEMENT; CLICHÉS; DENOTATION AND CONNOTATION; PARALLELISM; PUNCTUATION; REDUNDANCY AND REPETITION; SIMILAR WORDS; SPELLING; STYLE AND TONE

* * *

ELECTRONIC MAIL

Modern methods of communication involve creation of messages on computerized networks. The use of a local area network (LAN) is popular within corporations with one or more offices; some LANs are more public, with millions of possible users and hundreds of specialized modes for communication.

Most business users employ systems designed for limited access within a company, augmented by fax and LAN access outside the organization. Essentially, electronic mail (e-mail) is just that: messages developed on a word processing–style system and transferred to other employees of a company system. Messages—memos, letters, even longer reports—can be sent back and forth without the need to create hard copy. When such messages must be saved, electronic files are created for that purpose. The days when printouts dominated office space have passed with the widespread popularity of e-mail.

Two uses are of particular interest to the business user. First is the company-only e-mail system, in which communication is efficiently achieved without hard copy, photocopy, or manual distribution. A single message can be copied to as many addresses within the system as required, using a single keystroke rather than the time-consuming and expensive alternatives of the past. Second is the public user service, which provides encyclopedic-sized volumes of updated information on highly specialized topics. In combination, these two facilities provide business managers and executives with virtually immediate access to information both within the organization and from the outside.

The savings from the use of e-mail are substantial and can be seen immediately in lowered budgets for stationery, telephone, photocopying, and delivery expenses. Not visible in the departmental budget are the more significant savings, such as the advantage of instantaneous communications. The conveniences, however, also require safeguards and controls.

1.   Document communications decisions.

One potential flaw with any system that eases workload is the tendency to overlook important procedures. Document communications carefully using logs, saved files, and cross-references to be able to (1) rebuild the sequence of communications, (2) list those with whom you have shared your files, (3) recreate and retrieve important paperwork, and (4) update files without also losing the originals.

2.   Don't overlook the need for face-to-face meetings.

The popular use of electronic systems and other time-saving technologies does not entirely replace the need for face-to-face meetings. The human element can never be replaced entirely, and some matters are most effectively dealt with in meetings.

Avoid the temptation to replace direct contact through electronic alternatives completely.

3.   Design messages according to the situation.

Just as meetings are sometimes necessary, not every form of communication is best handled electronically. Some problems are readily solved with a personal discussion rather than through the exchange of written messages.

4.   Write topic lines correctly.

As e-mail grows in popularity, your message will have to compete with numerous others. The subject, or "entry," line for each message should be designed with these guidelines in mind:

a.   It should briefly and clearly state what the message contains.

A short, concise message is always more desirable than a longer, complex subject entry.

b.   It should get the reader's attention and interest.

Be a bit creative so that the message draws attention to itself.

Humdrum topic lines:
   Upcoming budget review meeting
   Fiscal analysis report, personal finance

Good topic lines:
   "Last chance" budget review—Tues. 10 a.m.
   Report: How *you* can save money

5. Remember the basics of good communication.

Electronic messages, like handwritten ones, must be designed with consideration for the basic requirements of style:

- Be brief and straightforward, with an emphasis on clarity.
- State early on the audience and purpose of communication, and end with an action plan, a request for response, and a signal that the message is over.
- If you are communicating with more than one person, limit and identify the audience.
- Avoid the temptation to clutter the e-mail of those who have no real interest in your message.

6. Edit prior to transmission.

Be sure to check your message before sending it. This review should not be limited to running it through a spell-checking system, although that is advisable as well. Read over what you have written, edit out any unnecessary parts, and look for ways to improve the style and clarity of your message.

*   *   *

Ellipses: *SEE* PUNCTUATION

EMPHASIS

Writers use emphasis to draw attention to key points in reports, letters, memos, and other documents.

1. Placement is the key.

The decision to place ideas provides an opportunity to emphasize what you consider the most important and to subordinate less important ideas. The key ideas should be expressed so that the reader understands the main idea.

Poor placement:
> The department has several tasks, including compliance,
> timely reporting, employee training, and, most
> important of all, cost controls.

Better placement:
> Cost control is the most important task in the department.
> Other tasks are compliance, timely reporting, and
> employee training.

In the second example, the item identified as most important is brought to the start of the paragraph, emphasizing it. Mentioning the key item first is not the only way to place the key sentence. In some cases, placing the key sentence elsewhere is just as effective.

Example:
> The department has a number of important tasks.
> However, every department has one job in common: cost
> control.

The concept of subordination is of equal importance in placement. Discussion of several items might obscure the point the writer is trying to make. By subordinating less important items, the writer allows the reader to concentrate on the major point. To subordinate a less important list, mention them after discussing the important or main point, or include the secondary items in parentheses or as a footnote.

2. Use repetition as a powerful expression tool.

The technique of repetition is extremely useful in conveying ideas. If overused, it becomes irritating, but selective emphasis of very important points is greatly aided with this device.

Effective repetition:
> Two-thirds of all customers stopped at the promotional
> display. Two-thirds.
> Our stores, like real estate, succeed or fail for three
> reasons: location, location, location.

Repetition of rhythm is another effective way to emphasize critical points. A three-point argument is a popular device, often used in promotional literature and annual reports. When you want to emphasize these points, use repetition and rhythm for maximum effect.

Three point repetition of rhythm:
We care about cost. We care about profit. We care about quality.
The organization aims to reduce cost, improve profit, and ensure quality.

A similar device to achieve emphasis is the contrary, or off-setting, statement.

Contrary statement:
We need to control our market, rather than allowing the market to control us.
Quality produces profits. Profits reflect quality.

3. Organize your opening and closing ideas.

Writers can use a technique public speakers practice to ensure that the important ideas are conveyed: open and close with the most important message. Some speakers subscribe to the three-step idea.

1. Tell them what you're going to say.
2. Say it.
3. Tell them what you said.

This might be too rudimentary for reporting within the business environment, where brevity is appreciated; however, the point is well made.

Example:
Customer loyalty is the key. Once the customer accepts the pricing, service, and quality we provide, we have earned that customer's loyalty. However, if we establish that and then betray the customer's faith, we will never recapture it. We have to deserve loyalty, and we have to keep it. That loyalty is the key.

4. Be aware of the appearance of your message.

The way you design your message has much to do with how it is received. Like other techniques of emphasis, overuse destroys the intended result. Some of these design elements include:

s p a c i n g
italics
<u>underlining</u>
CAPITALIZATION
words in "quotation marks"

You may also isolate a limited amount of text and enclose it in a box as a sidebar to a report, as a form of emphasis.

Just changing the margins and
spacing of a single sentence
achieves the same result.

If you attempt to emphasize too much of your message, you lose the effect. Also avoid using too many stylistic methods for emphasis within a single report or letter. When a single **report** contains <u>too many</u> STYLE t y p e s, the reader will be distracted.

5. Insert headings for emphasis.

In preparing reports, label sections clearly as a form of emphasis. Many people on the distribution list will not want to read the entire report but might be interested in selected portions. By providing headings, you make their task easier.

You may also provide headings in letters, memos, and other documents. They break up lengthy documents into smaller sections and help the reader quickly identify the sections of the document.

6. Use visual aids effectively.

Charts and graphs are efficient devices for emphasis. Important statistical information can be reduced to a half-page in the form of a graph, and the important point can be conveyed instantly to the reader. Without visual aids for such key information, the reader will need to visualize and translate narrative information without help. The message may not be conveyed at all.

The use of color is an additional way to emphasize a key point. This may include colorized charts and graphs or the use of a highlighter pen.

7.   Insert lists and outlines to break up text.

Business reporting is concerned more with agenda items and priorities than with narrative and descriptive text. Accordingly, lists and outlines are appropriate forms. These techniques also provide excellent opportunities for emphasis. Whenever dealing with several important topics in the same report, use the outline form in the report's body to lead the reader through. Use lists to draw attention to the critical and major elements in a decision.

8.   Insert dashes, commas, and parentheses for variety in emphasis.

Be aware of the relative degree of emphasis achieved in selection of methods for asides or secondary thoughts. The greatest emphasis is achieved by setting material between dashes; commas provide somewhat less emphasis; and parentheses tend to downplay the separate word or other material, providing the least amount of emphasis.

> *Examples:*
> During the period of civil unrest—four days—our stores were closed by government decree.
> The results of the survey, impressive and promising, were nonetheless conducted in a flawed manner.
> Our entire purpose (increasing market share) was shattered by the competition's development of a cheaper, better product.

9.   Design sentences to achieve clarity and emphasis.

The construction of a sentence determines its clarity. Edit your own writing to clarify your intended message. When a sentence's meaning is unclear, chances are it should be broken into two sentences or that some words can be removed without losing the meaning.

Unclear message:

> Priorities within the department itself can be categorized in two major groups, immediate and long term, both of which depend on budgetary constraints and approval from top management before we can proceed.

Clearer message:

> Departmental priorities depend on budgetary constraint and approval from top management. These restrictions apply to both immediate and long-term priorities.

A second feature to be aware of in design of sentences is *rhythm*. When a reader is exposed to a long paragraph containing sentences of the same length, the monotony may cause him or her to lose concentration and perhaps not retain the information fully.

Monotonous rhythm:

> Every division has experienced budget problems. Attempts at solving them have had mixed results. New controls are probably called for. Centralized management has not been effective in this effort. More action is needed at the divisional level.

Variations in rhythm:

> Every division has experienced budget problems, along with mixed results in attempted solutions. New controls are required, but centralized management has not been effective in this effort. Divisional-level action is the answer.

Vary the length of paragraphs to achieve the same variety in rhythm. When paragraphs are consistently seven to eight lines long, the entire document becomes a difficult-to-read, monotonous reading chore. Consider one-sentence paragraphs to add high emphasis to a key point. (Note: As a general rule, a true paragraph should not contain only one sentence. As a technique for achieving emphasis, that rule can be broken occasionally.)

See also: ACTIVE AND PASSIVE VOICE; DENOTATION AND CONNOTATION; HEADINGS; HIGHLIGHTING IN TEXT; PARAGRAPHS

* * *

Exclamation Mark: *SEE* PUNCTUATION

FALSE SUBJECTS

A false subject is an abstract pronoun. Often found at the beginning of sentences, false subjects weaken the tone of the message. A false subject damages the sentence because it replaces the intended subject with the indefinite article. Occasionally, however, you may wish to use a false subject deliberately.

1. Identify false subjects.

Know how to recognize a false subject. Being able to spot their use helps break bad habits, and helps you to train yourself to avoid them.

False subjects:
It is our intention to meet this afternoon.
This *report* is the most critical of the reports.

Actual subjects:
> We intend to meet this afternoon.
> This is the most critical report.

2.   Edit out the false subject.

Correcting the problem of false subjects invariably involves removal of unnecessary words. Accordingly, the task is fairly straightforward compared to other editorial problems. Look out for sentences beginning with phrases such as *It is, It was, There is,* and *There was.* The indefinite pronouns in these examples (*It* and *There*) are readily identified false subjects. Your writing style will improve dramatically if you learn to weed them out from the beginnings of your sentences. False subjects also appear in the middle of sentences, so merely looking for the problem at the beginnings will not capture all instances.

Mid-sentence false subjects:
> We decided that it would be necessary to prepare a
> written explanation.

Corrected sentence:
> We decided to prepare a written explanation.

3.   Leave in false subjects when necessary.

Sometimes false subjects have to be left in a sentence because of the way they are used. The language allows for some appropriate false subjects, a feature that maintains its richness and variety. In editing, recognize that some false subjects should be left in place.

Necessary false subjects:
> It was five P.M., so work stopped for the day.
> There is no evidence to support that theory.

*   *   *

FINANCIAL REPORTS

The most common form of reporting in business is financial. The most reliable way to measure performance is through analysis of profit and loss, cash flow, and the relationship between assets and liabilities. A manager seeking approval for new equipment or a change in processes has the highest probability of success when presenting arguments based on financial projections. Large organizations make great effort in budgeting and forecasting and on monitoring results to check the accuracy and reliability of those budgets.

Accountants deal with the major financial reporting and budgeting functions in most companies, but all managers and employees can improve their skills in communication by mastering the style points for financial reporting.

1. Avoid excessive narrative discussion of numbers.

Reports often attempt to combine large volumes of numerical data with accompanying narrative explanations. Some report writers make the mistake of believing the narrative sections should repeat the numbers, even though the numbers are plainly self-evident. Use narrative sections to discuss ideas and goals or to explain to the reader the nonnumerical aspects of the case while avoiding redundant references to charts, graphs, and tables.

Redundant narrative:

The accompanying table shows that 26 percent of gross profits are paid out in salaries; 47 percent to other overhead; 22 percent to taxes; and only 5 percent remain in the form of net profits.

Concise narrative:

> Results for the year (see Table 1) break down the gross
> profit by category. Although only 5 percent of gross
> ends up on the bottom line, this result is an
> improvement over the previous year.

In the second example, the same amount of space is used to make a significant point for the reader. Because the table contains the breakdown, it is unnecessary to repeat what is already shown.

2.   Use charts and graphs to make financial reporting arguments visual.

Large volumes of numbers are difficult to explain; no one readily perceives the real significance of long columns and rows of numbers unless they are extremely familiar with the issue, and many readers of reports do not have the benefit of such knowledge. The report writer has to determine the most efficient style for conveying information.

3.   Use tables with text, and discuss their significance.

Charts and graphs can be used to reduce a full page of difficult-to-understand numbers to the essential conclusions they show. The visual representation is invariably more effective than any narrative. Reserve narrative sections to interpret what the numbers reveal.

4.   Emphasize important conclusions with percentages.

In narrative sections, convey conclusions rather than passively repeat numbers. When you do need to discuss the values, however, express them as percentages rather than numerically.

Numeric expression:
> Sales last quarter were $1.65 million, and net profits
> were $115,500.

Clearer message using percentages:
> Net profits last year were 7 percent of sales.

5. Follow reporting conventions.

Financial reporting follows a standard format, both in reporting style and in the arrangement of reports and accompanying charts and graphs. Because of the precise nature of the accounting report, these formatting conventions and styles are to be followed strictly.

This does not mean, however, that the report should be unnecessarily technical or difficult to understand. Remember that the reader is not always well-versed in accounting terminology or style. Here are some additional suggested guidelines to add to the clarity of financial reports:

1. Attach explanatory notes for the reader who lacks an accounting background and who may need to be oriented to essential, important information.
2. Use footnotes when appropriate to draw the reader's attention to unusual or especially significant information.
3. Use financial reports as tools that enhance a less formal verbal report, which is always preferable when communicating numerical information.
4. Encourage everyone in the organization to use financial terminology in a consistent manner. If necessary, publish an internal summary of special jargon to help clarify communication.

See also: CHARTS AND GRAPHS; DECIMALS, FRACTIONS, AND PERCENTAGES

*   *   *

FLOWCHARTS

Processing information at the departmental level requires complete documentation of procedures: instructions for reporting, use of forms, departments and individuals to use as sources and to whom results are sent, the reporting chain, and numerous other related ideas. Department supervisors are invariably responsible for setting up a system to document the processes completed in their department. Part of that assignment includes listing the steps and routines related to every task and procedure. One tool that is useful in this task is the flowchart.

1. Use the rudimentary single-process flowchart for single-process ideas.

The most basic format for flowcharting follows one line of steps. For this reason, we call it the *single-process flowchart* (Figure F-1). This format became popular in the 1960s and 1970s, when flowcharting became associated with computer science. Because a computer executes only one function at a time within a single routine, the flow of logic is best shown by way of a single-process flowchart.

The decision box is shaped differently from others and represents the point in the process where a loop occurs. In this example, a "yes" answer to the question returns the flow to the previous box. When a "no" answer appears, the flow continues onward.

2. Use differently shaped boxes to represent different functions.

A wide variety of box shapes were developed within the computer industry to represent different functions. Use differently shaped boxes in the single-process flowchart for the same purpose, although limit the number of varieties to avoid confusion.

Figure F-1. Single-Process Flowchart: Name Verification Routine

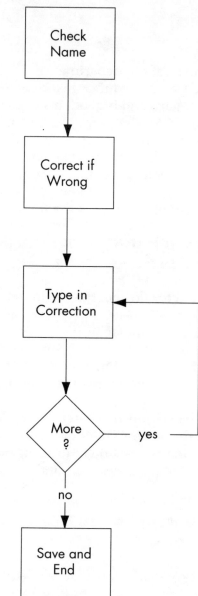

Figure F-2. Dynamic Flowchart

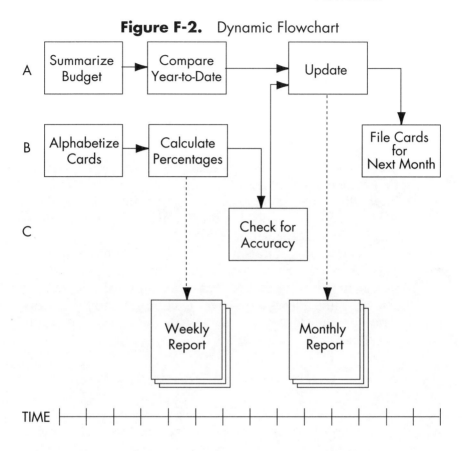

You may need different shapes for process steps, decisions, documents, and start or finish.

3. Use the dynamic flowchart for multiprocess ideas.

While computer programs execute steps in order, human processing is often vastly different. In the business environment, managers and employees rarely work in isolation. Typically several people in different departments contribute segments to a larger process. In documenting human processes, the *dynamic flowchart* makes more sense (Figure F-2).

This format presents a practical style for documenting processes in the noncomputer world. The same chart shows three different departments, labeled A, B, and C, each executing a number of steps in the simplified process. There is interaction among the departments, shown by the sequence lines and arrows. Also shown are the documents produced as part of the process, represented by the dotted lines below the departmental flow, and the time line indicated along the bottom. The advantages of using the dynamic flowchart include the following:

- The processes in different departments are shown in relation to one another.
- Interaction among departments is documented. These are the most likely points for breakdown in procedures, so this feature is especially valuable.
- The documents produced as part of the procedure are important to the trainee and to the manager responsible for producing reports, forms, and other types of documents.
- The time line allows a reviewer to comprehend the importance of interdepartmental flow in the context of deadlines.

4.   Design procedures manuals around the flowchart.

The dynamic flowchart is an excellent tool for the development of thorough documentation. When developing a procedures manual, begin with the dynamic flowchart, and then add narratives to support it. This method is preferable to the more common one of developing manuals with narratives only, making it difficult for employee trainees to comprehend the larger picture. By working from a flowchart, the manual developer is forced to account for every step in the process, as well as for methods by which information flows among departments.

See also: ORGANIZATION CHARTS; PROCEDURES MANUALS

*   *   *

FOOTNOTES

1. Add footnotes for clarification as a comment that is relevant to the primary topic though not part of it.

The format is to make a noted reference in the text, and place the footnote at the bottom of that same page. Notes may be denoted by an asterisk or a number.

> *Anecdotal information:*
>> The difficulty of communicating directly often leads to less direct means of expression.*
>
> ---
>
> *One manager, cited by Harmon, 1993, got the message across to a chronically tardy employee by locking the door from the parking lot at five minutes past starting time.

2. Insert a footnote to the source of specific information or when you quote from another source.

> *Statistical information that supports a comment in text:*
>> The majority of managers cite the problem of absenteeism as their primary concern in the department.[1]
>
> ---
>
> 1. Survey of 126 managers, University of Saratoga, 1994.

> *Source material for a quotation or fragment, or a limited fact:*
>> The "frustrated manager" expresses his frustration not overtly, but in other ways.*
>
> ---
>
> *Harmon 1993.

A recent study revealed that a scant 13 percent of
business managers had even read the procedures
manual.[11]

---

11. Ames, 1995.

3. Follow the correct format for listing sources.

a. Book citations.

1. Author: The author is given first, as listed on the title
page. When more than three authors are listed, the first author's
name is followed by "et al." When the listed authors are editors,
their names are followed by "eds."

2. Title: The title of the book follows, in italics.

3. Publication information: This information is presented parenthetically in the following order: city of publication,
plus the state abbreviation if the city is obscure; publisher's
name; and date.

4. Page references: The page references that the material appears on is the final information.

Citations for books:

Wendy Evans et al., *Border Crossings* (Scarborough,
    Ont.: Prentice-Hall Canada, 1992), pp. 113–114.
Frank Fisher and Carmen Sirianni, eds., *Critical Studies in
    Organization and Bureaucracy* (Philadelphia: Temple
    University Press, 1984), p. 53.
Michael C. Thomsett, *The Little Black Book of Business
    Math* (New York: Amacom, 1988), pp. 72–79.

Subsequent references to the same work in the document
use a shortened form of the citation:

Shortened book citations:
> Evans et al., *Border Crossings,* p. 53.
> Fisher and Sirianni, eds., *Critical Studies,* p. 16.

b. Magazine, periodical, and newspaper citations:

The format for citing articles in newspapers and magazines is similar to that of books; however, the article title or headline is included as well as the main publication title. In addition, the publication volume number, month of publication, and page numbers are included. For a newspaper or other periodical published other than monthly, the precise date is given.

Magazine citation:
> Nicholas Lemann, "The Structure of Success in America," *Atlantic Monthly* 51 (August 1995): 41.

Newspaper:
> David Warsh, "Manufacturing in Massachusetts," *Boston Globe,* October 3, 1995, p. 68.

Subsequent references to the same work in the document use a shortened form of the citation:

Shortened magazine article citation:
> Lemann, "Structure of Success," p. 31.

Shortened newspaper citation:
> Warsh, "Manufacturing," p. 68.

c. Unpublished works:

Follow the same format for published works to the degree possible: author, title, source, year.

Citations of unpublished works:
> Martha Brown, "Solving the Automated Transition Problem" (speech presented at Ames Corp. seminar, February 24, 1996). J. Green, letter to the author, May 17, 1995.

4. Use "ibid." when the same source is cited consecutively.

5. If the document has a bibliography, the citation in the footnote can list only the author, date, and page number.

Example:

---

3. Harmon 1993, p. 31.

When you use this format, a full citation must appear in the bibliography.

6. Use footnotes only when they are absolutely necessary.

Footnotes are useful and interesting when appropriate; they can be entertaining as well, and can be used effectively to break up the rhythm of a report or study. However, excessive footnoting can also become disruptive and distracting to the flow of the document.

See also: CITATIONS

*   *   *

Fractions: *SEE* DECIMALS, FRACTIONS, AND PERCENTAGES

HEADINGS

Reports and other documents longer than a single page are often difficult for readers to absorb. Not all of the material is of interest to everyone; and time limitations may prevent the reader from devoting the time necessary to the entire document. Headings break up the text and allow the reader to concentrate on selective parts.

1. Provide a guide to the sections.

When presenting complex material in a report, break it down into logical components, and give each section a meaningful heading. On the report's Table of Contents, list these headings and their page numbers.

This situation comes up in lengthy reports. You will probably deal with wide-ranging subject matter in a comprehensive report, and a Table of Contents that lists headings makes the reader's task easier. A potential reader who might be interested in only certain parts is more likely to look at the report if it has numbered pages and provides convenient cross-references.

2. Use headings for documents that are several pages long.

Headings help readers when the document exceeds a few pages. Even a single topic can be broken down into logical sections. Readers like heading breaks because the segmentation enables them to absorb the subject. Heading breaks are similar to chapter breaks in a book.

3. Use headings for multiple ideas.

Headings make particular sense when a single document discusses more than one idea because they alert readers that the subject is changing. If the reader has to read back over material to figure out what is being discussed, it will usually be at the expense of comprehension.

4. Use emphasis and placement to draw the reader's attention to headings.

Headings can be expressed in several ways. When you have a large number of headings, they may be numbered or given alphabetical distinctions. Placement and style also make the heading distinctive. Centering the heading in the report ensures its identification as a heading. If you have both primary and secondary headings, treat each type consistently in the same manner.

>   *Heading treatment:*
>   —The Quarterly Budget—
>   THE QUARTERLY BUDGET
>   *The Quarterly Budget*
>   **The Quarterly Budget**
>   The Quarterly Budget

5. Keep titles of headings brief but informative.

Avoid overly long headings. A heading that exceeds one line (or is close to a full line in length) loses its distinctiveness. If such length is unavoidable, center it on two single-spaced lines, and break the lines so that the words that are grouped make sense.

>   *Two-line heading:*
>   Quarterly Budget Variances
>   and Proposed Solutions

Shorter headings are invariably better choices than the example. The heading does not have to cover the topic comprehensibly; it only needs to provide a guideline about the general topic. Remember that readers want to be able to skim through the document and concentrate on areas of particular interest. The shorter the heading is, the easier this task will be.

>   *Variations on a single heading:*
>   Budget Variance Solutions
>   Variance Solutions
>   Solutions

See also: CAPTIONS; REPORTS

*   *   *

Highlighting in Text

Emphasis requires drawing attention to a word or phrase within the text. Methods include capitalization, boldface, italics, and underlining.

1.   Capitalize for selective emphasis.

Use all caps for single words only, and apply this method sparingly. Excessive use of capital letters tends to give the appearance of unnecessary alarm, in some cases, even appearing as a form of exaggeration. In addition, lengthy passages in all caps can be difficult to read.

> *Excessive use:*
> This year's NET PROFITS are HIGHER than projected.

> *Preferred, limited use:*
> This year's net profits are HIGHER than projected.

Use of capital letters should be extremely limited. The most common purpose is for acronyms.

> *Acronym expression:*
> The company's stock is listed on NASDAQ under the symbol ABBS.

Some word processors offer the option of small caps, easier to read than all caps in headlines or titles. Do not, however, use the small-caps feature for acronyms.

> *Small caps:*
> Marketing Department Business Plan

2. Utilize boldface.

Using **boldface type** is a better way to emphasize than capitalization. Word processing systems and electronic typewriters can
print in boldface type. Use boldface for the following reasons:

- Highlighting of key words or limited phrases.
- Distinction for different levels of headings and subheadings when working in outline form.

3. Utilize italics and underlining.

Like boldface, word processing systems and electronic typewriters can print in *italic type.* When working on a system that does
not have italic typeface, writers underline words in text, indicating to the typesetter that the word should be italicized.

a. Use italics or underlining to provide spe-cial emphasis to part of a quotation.

Be sure to indicate that *you* are adding italics in this situation.

Example:
> The article pointed out that "the study found *no instances*
> of failure in the marketing plan [italics added]."

b. Use italics or underlining to emphasize a single word or short phrase in a report or let-ter that requires special attention from the reader or that you want to point out.

Example:
> Our division is *not* considering the plan.

c. Use italics or underlining for foreign words and phrases that are not part of the everyday English language.

Example:
> The team leader has veto power *ex officio.*

d. Use italics or underlining for words used as examples within text.

Example:
> How should we distinguish between the words *farther* and *further* in our reports?

4. Apply general guidelines for emphasis.

a. Restraint:

Use highlighted words and phrases selectively. Remember that overemphasizing distracts the reader and destroys the desired effect. If you are tempted to use too much emphasis, perhaps you are not confident the text expresses your message clearly. Self-edit to improve text before resorting to highlighting for emphasis.

b. Consistency of form:

Use highlighting consistently within a single document. Do not switch between, say, boldface and italics for similar or identical phrases used several times within one report. Select one style of highlighting, and stay with it.

c. Choice of form:

Pick the form of highlighting that works best for the type of document and the type of use. Perhaps you think that boldface will appear excessive, so you choose to use italics or underlining. Or you may think italics looks too timid and prefer boldface.

Boldface for key word emphasis:
> Seminar topics include **management** and **leadership** in a remote office environment.

d. Singularity of form:

Avoid combining two or more forms of highlighting. Readers are distracted by combined uses. A properly used highlighting technique should appear logical and correct within the text and should not unduly draw the reader's attention.

See also: EMPHASIS

*   *   *

Hyphen: *SEE* PUNCTUATION

Italics: *SEE* HIGHLIGHTING IN TEXT

INTRODUCTIONS

Introductions are placed at the beginnings of reports, to orient readers to the contents.

1.   Keep the introduction short.

Introductions are not intended to become a major section of the report. They should be kept as short as possible and limited in scope. Long introductions will not be read all the way through; most readers want to get to the heart of the report as quickly as possible.

2.   Use introductions only for long documents.

If you have prepared a relatively short report, no introduction is required. Also avoid introductions for nonreport documents. They are useful only for orienting readers of longer reports, procedures and policy manuals, and studies.

3.   Summarize critical information.

The introduction is the best place to list information you consider the most critical.

a. The conclusion or major recommendation:

Always start a report with the most important conclusion. The reader is then prepared to look through the report to examine supporting documentation, methods, and other material. Be sure to repeat the most important conclusion in the first section in case the reader skips the introduction, a not-uncommon situation.

b. The statistical or research methods used:

Any report drawing conclusions should document the sources used. You may have developed your own research or used statistical information from other sources. In either event, briefly summarize these facts in the Introduction. For extensively used statistics or research, plan also to provide greater details and supporting information in an appendix to the report.

c. The reason for the document's preparation:

Readers who are unfamiliar with your purpose or intention might not immediately grasp the purpose of the report. Explain this in the introduction. Assume, for example, you are preparing a report to ask management to purchase a new machine for your department. You prepare a report proving that the investment will save time and money, enabling the company to recapture its investment in a short period of time. Set out this purpose in the introduction.

d. Special considerations important to readers:

Some reports contain information, sources, or statistical studies not commonly used, or they may involve an unusual method. In such cases, be sure to summarize these considerations for the reader.

e. Scope of the report, if exceptional:

Some reports are very limited in scope, prepared on assignment for one individual. Others are distributed to a wide array of readers. Explain the scope of your report in the introduction.

f.   References to other important documents:

Reports may refer to other reports prepared within the company; to material prepared by other companies or by government agencies; or to published material in books, research magazines, or trade publications. Refer to these in the introduction if they are limited in scope. If you have used a wide range of sources, explain the range in the introduction and include a bibliography of sources at the back of the report.

g.   The involvement of other individuals or departments:

If the report is a multidepartmental effort, be certain to acknowledge the participation of all others in the project. This is a courtesy to the others who worked on the report; it may also be important information, letting the reader know that more than one point of view was considered by the report preparer.

4.   Write the introduction last.

Regardless of the sequence in which your document was prepared, the introduction should be written last. Only upon completion of the report will you know all of the critical points that should be contained in the introduction.

See also: CITATIONS; REPORTS

*   *   *

JARGON

In the business world, a language trap is the tendency to use language poorly or to develop the habit of expressing ideas in unique ways. This tendency leads to poor style habits. Jargon is highly technical or specialized language unique to a special profession—for example, law, engineering, and accounting—or even within a single corporation or office.

1. Be aware of the dangers of excessive jargon.

Employees in an organization spend most of their time with fellow employees and develop certain words and phrases as a kind of shorthand. Be aware of which terms may be unique to the organization. If they are used outside the immediate organization, communication may be impeded.

2. Create a glossary for highly specialized terms.

When developing training materials, reports to those outside the occupation (including management), and even reports to fellow employees, define terms that may be unfamiliar to the reader. If your occupation uses jargon extensively, compile a glossary and distribute it to others. Avoid the unintentional consequence of unexplained jargon: a tendency to isolate yourself from all others who are not in your occupation.

3. Define technical terms when they first come up.

A good practice is to define technical terms the first time they are used in reports, letters, and other documents. Definitions can often be inserted in text without distracting the reader or taking up excessive space. This practice clarifies the report for the reader.

4. Avoid technical terms as much as possible.

When preparing a document for an individual outside your occupation or when writing a letter or memo for wide distribution, avoid using special terms or technical expressions. Remember that such terms are developed for the convenience of those working in the field, and outsiders cannot be expected to comprehend them. Avoiding technical terms and striving for clarity of expression will benefit your readers.

5. Recognize obscure expression.

A related problem is to write in obscure terms. Even those who are not technical writers may fall into this trap. In the interest of clarity, the less obscurely you write, the better. Jargon develops as a bad habit because, in the corporate environment, the practice of communicating indirectly becomes easier than making short, direct statements.

> *An obscure statement:*
>
> Departmental management contends and establishes its position that investment in this program will contribute to the development of greater profits in the immediate future.

> *A clearer communication:*
>
> The manager proved that investing in this program will be profitable within a year.

6. Find the shortest way to say it.

Edit for brevity as one method for avoiding obscure statements. As a general rule, the shortest way to say something is also the clearest way.

> *Unedited statement:*
>
> If your schedule is not otherwise committed at this point in time, I would be interested in arranging for a midday respite meeting with you on the first day of the coming week.

> *Shorter, clearer statement:*
>
> Are you free for lunch on Monday?

7. Self-edit for clarity of style.

Get into the practice of editing your own work before sending it to others. Use these methods to improve your clarity:

- Seek the shortest word with the same meaning.
- Limit letters and memos to one page when possible.
- Remove any material not absolutely essential to your message.
- In a report, remove highly detailed discussions and, if they are necessary, put them in an appendix.

See also: CLICHÉS; EDITING AND PROOFREADING

* * *

LETTERS

A primary method for communicating in the business world is the letter. Letters make a first impression and often introduce the entire organization. When the first contact an outsider has with a company is a letter, the writing style, spelling, and style convey an impression about the entire company. A single error or careless statement can destroy goodwill or create suspicion and mistrust. In contrast, a well-written, clearly expressed message strengthens the company's reputation, as well as the reputation of the writer.

1. Take special care with outside communications.

The business letter is the first impression you make for your organization. Whenever you correspond, the way you express yourself and the appearance of the letter together create an idea in someone else's mind about your company and you. If that image is positive, it benefits the company; if negative, it can do permanent harm.

As a rule of thumb, always assume that individuals outside the organization will send a copy of your correspondence to your company president. Would you worry about the impression you create? Or would you be confident that the way you express yourself and the appearance of your letter make the best possible impression?

2.   Arrange the letter correctly.

Many style points have to do with the kind of impression your letters make. Seemingly small matters, like the size of columns and space left at the bottom of the page, make a big difference. Someone who receives a letter from you consciously or unconsciously makes an immediate judgment about you and your organization based on the overall appearance of the letter. All of the details that go into proper construction of the correspondence matter, because each adds to the overall impression: construction and style, spelling (especially the name of the person you are writing to), the size and amount of margins allowed in the letter, and where on the page you place the address, the date, and the salutation.

Arrangement also refers to the contents of each segment of the letter. Deferring for the moment a discussion of the set-up, consider the importance of the three sections in the body of the letter:

a.   First paragraph:

The opening paragraph determines whether the reader will go through the entire letter and to what degree your message will be well received. The first paragraph should summarize your key point, attract the reader's interest and attention, and explain exactly what the letter is concerned with.

b.   Body of the letter:

Within the main body of the letter, provide specific recommendations, requests, ideas, and other important points. All letters should be just as long as they need to be. As a rule, any business document has a greater chance of being read if it is short rather than long.

c. Last paragraph:

Reserve the last paragraph for your closing argument: a request, a question, a promise, or a summary of important information. If the letter's intention is to ask for something, ask the question here.

> *Poorly constructed last paragraph:*
>
> In conclusion and to respond to your inquiry, our company's products are summarized in the enclosed catalog. We hope you will find it interesting.

> *Improved last paragraph:*
>
> Our catalog is enclosed. I hope you will look at it right away, and I appreciate your interest. Would you like to place an order?

3. Select the right length for the letter.

Every letter has its appropriate length. When the length begins to exceed three or four pages, it might be a report rather than a letter, meaning it should be organized in a different format and accompanied by a relatively short introductory letter.

The most desirable length for a letter is one page or less because the reader is less likely to read longer letters than shorter ones. Any message can be expressed briefly as long as supporting materials can be enclosed separately. Where letters exceed a single page, strive for clarity of expression. Where possible, summarize multiple-part discussions in outline form so that the reader will be able to seek out specific points or tell at a glance the points your letter makes.

Letters can be kept fairly short even for complex topics. Enclose supporting material to keep the letter brief and directed. For example, if your letter is on the topic of an eight-point argument based on a series of statistical tests, summarize the eight points in the body of the letter and refer to the supporting material. The key point is this: the letter is most effective if it is used to direct the reader to the most pertinent sections of the enclosed material. It will be least effective if the same space is used to try to summarize a complex series of arguments.

4. Observe style conventions consistently.

You have a variety of style choices in setting up letter formats. However, some conventions are more widely accepted for professional correspondence.

a. Address and dates:

Placement of addresses and dates, as well as other margin alternatives, depend first on letterhead style. If your company's letterhead is arranged on the left top side of the page, the letter will appear more balanced if the date is indented on the left. If letterhead style takes up the entire top or is centered, you have greater flexibility in style.

Block style is the most conventional letter form: all material in the letter shares a common margin on the left side of the page. That means that the date, address, salutation, each paragraph, the closing, and the signature block have the same margin. If the company's logo or name lines up to the left, the placement of the margin should conform to the left edge of that printed material.

The correct format for dates is as follows:

1. The month comes first, and should be spelled out completely.
2. The date, in numerals, is next, followed by a comma.
3. The year, in numerals, is last, and is not abbreviated; all four digits are included.

Incorrect date styles:
16 February, 1996
8 Jan. 1997
23 March '97

Correct date styles:
February 16, 1996
January 8, 1997
March 23, 1997

On all pages beyond page 1, blocks at the top of the page may include the name of the person to whom the letter is addressed, the date, and the page number. The date may be spelled out (e.g., September 19, 1996) or abbreviated in numerical form (e.g., 9/19/96).

Address blocks contain the full name and title of the person to whom the letter is addressed; the full address on the second line; the city, abbreviation of state, possession or province, and postal code on the third line. When abbreviating states, possessions, and provinces, use a two-letter abbreviation in all-caps; do not punctuate with periods. Correct postal abbreviations are shown in Table L-1.

b. Attention line:

Some letters are addressed to an organization rather than to an individual, with an "attention line" directed to a department, a title, or an individual. This is the appropriate format to use when the person's name is not known or when you know the name but prefer to address your letter to the department. In the name and address block, the company name is listed but no individual or department. Follow this with the attention line.

Examples:
   Attention: Customer Service Department
   Attention: J. Davis, Account Supervisor
   Attention: Vice President, Sales

c. Reference line:

After the address, the subject of the letter is summarized in the reference line, a brief descriptive phrase advising the reader of the letter's topic.

Examples:
   Re: Budget Committee report
   Re: Sales meeting agenda
   Re: Coding errors, acct. 4475

d. Salutation:

The proper form for salutation in letters differs from that used in memos, notes, and other forms of correspondence. The letter

Table L-1. Postal Abbreviations

United States:

Alabama	AL	Montana	MT
Alaska	AK	Nebraska	NB
Arizona	AZ	Nevada	NV
Arkansas	AR	New Hampshire	NH
California	CA	New Jersey	NJ
Colorado	CO	New Mexico	NM
Connecticut	CT	New York	NY
Delaware	DE	North Carolina	NC
District of Columbia	DC	North Dakota	ND
Florida	FL	Ohio	OH
Georgia	GA	Oklahoma	OK
Guam	GU	Oregon	OR
Hawaii	HI	Pennsylvania	PA
Idaho	ID	Puerto Rico	PR
Illinois	IL	Rhode Island	RI
Indiana	IN	South Carolina	SC
Iowa	IA	South Dakota	SD
Kansas	KS	Tennessee	TN
Kentucky	KY	Texas	TX
Louisiana	LA	Utah	UT
Maine	ME	Vermont	VT
Maryland	MD	Virginia	VA
Massachusetts	MA	Virgin Islands	VI
Michigan	MI	Washington	WA
Minnesota	MN	West Virginia	WV
Mississippi	MS	Wisconsin	WI
Missouri	MO	Wyoming	WY

Canada:

Alberta	AB	Nova Scotia	NS
British Columbia	BC	Ontario	ON
Labrador	LB	Prince Edward Island	PE
Manitoba	MB	Quebec	PQ
New Brunswick	NB	Saskatchewan	SK
Newfoundland	NF	Yukon Territory	YT
Northwest Territories	NT		

normally is addressed to the individual by name, preceded by the word *Dear*. In a formal letter, include the individual's identifying honorific: *Mr., Mrs.,* or *Ms.* After the name, place a colon.

Formal salutation:
Dear Mr. Sanders:
Dear Mrs. Adams:
Dear Ms. Thomas:

Use first names when you are on a first-name basis with the individual.

Informal salutation:
Dear Bob:
Dear Amy:

In some cases, you may be unsure whether an individual is male or female, either because the name may be either or because only initials are provided. In these cases, the salutation should include the entire name.

Salutation when gender is not known:
Dear Leslie Black:
Dear M. W. Haroldson:

When writing to a group of people rather than to an individual, make the salutation all inclusive.

Salutation to a group:
Dear Gentlemen or Ladies:
Dear Finance Committee:
Dear Executive Committee:

e. Closing and signature line:

The closing segment of the letter is a short section of one to four words followed by a comma, intended to end the letter with the right tone or flavor to the message. The closing should be appropriate for a business communication and is based on the formality or informality of the relationship. If you, as letter writer, are a peer and close friend of the individual to whom the letter is sent, the closing can be correspondingly informal.

Informal closings:
  As always,
  Your friend,
  Best wishes,

However, if the letter is to a superior, an individual or a group outside the organization, or someone you have not met, a more formal closing should be used.

Formal closings:
  Sincerely,
  Cordially,
  With regards,

Your name should be typed and aligned directly under the closing, leaving adequate room for your written signature—usually about four spaces. Put your name only without any punctuation. Whenever practical, sign the letter yourself in ink. Avoid the use of rubber stamps or having someone else sign your name and placing their initials after the signature. That is a proper practice but not very personal, and could convey the idea that this letter was not important to you.

The closing and signature should be put at the same margin with the date and address blocks. When using block style, this would be at the far left margin on the page.

f. Letterhead and envelope:

Always use a business envelope and business letterhead when corresponding in the name of the company. Internal correspondence can be executed far less formally, but all letters sent outside the office should be done on preprinted letter and envelope forms.

If your company has more than one letterhead style, your letter and envelope should be of the same style. Do not mix your letter with a different envelope.

The address on the envelope should always be typed, centered in the middle of the envelope and identical to the address as it appears on the letter. Several formats may be used (for letters *and* envelopes) when directing the letter to the attention of one individual within an organization or department. The style should match on both letter and envelope.

Address formats:

Ms. Marjorie Abbott, Manager
The Ames Company
804 Third Avenue
New York, NY 10022

The Ames Company
Attn: Ms. Marjorie Abbott, Manager
804 Third Avenue
New York, NY 10022

The Ames Company
804 Third Avenue
New York, NY 10022
Attn: Ms. Marjorie Abbott, Manager

In the final example, the *Attn:* box should be placed several lines below the address block and to the left. Either of the first two formats is more acceptable than the third one.

g. Block style:

The block style is the most common format for business letters and, in many respects, the most desirable. Because it is commonly used, other businesspeople may expect to see the clean, professional, and simple format in which all lines, including each paragraph, are aligned to the left.

For this style, do not justify the right margin, even if you are using a word processing system that provides the justifying feature. Justification on both right and left tends to give the letter too much of a cubed appearance. Styles with indented paragraphs may seem to take on an improved appearance with justification, but the block style does not.

With block style, paragraphs are not indented; a line is

skipped between paragraphs. Similarly, all other segments of the letter—date, address, attention line, reference line, salutation, closing, and signature—are aligned on the same left margin.

h. Modified, semiblock, and simplified styles:

1. *Modified block style* follows most of the same rules as the standard block style, except that date, reference lines, closing, and signature are placed to the right of the page's center. The effect is still blocklike, but the left margin paragraphs are offset by these other items, giving the page slightly more balance.

2. *The semiblock style* also calls for placing some segments to the right of page center, as with modified block. However, paragraphs are indented rather than a line being skipped (the indent is normally five type spaces).

3. *Simplified style* is rarer. The salutation and closing lines are excluded altogether, so that the letter lacks even the minimal effort at adding a personal touch. Modern custom rarely calls for the use of simplified style.

i. Punctuation guidelines for letter style:

1. *For standard style,* only absolutely necessary punctuation is used. A colon (or sometimes a comma) is placed after the salutation. A comma is included after the closing and before the signature space. In the letter itself, standard punctuation rules apply.

2. *Closed style* is an outdated convention in which all punctuation is included, including periods after dates and commas after each line of the address. This style is unacceptable today. The closed style draws attention to itself and gives a letter an unprofessional appearance.

j. Margins and spacing:

Margins on the left and right should be about the same width. On word processing systems, they can be set permanently for all correspondence. A margin of $1\frac{1}{4}$ inches provides enough white space to give the letter a professional appearance. The margin size is sometimes dictated by the company's letterhead design and logo placement. If the preprinted matter begins 1 inch from the far left edge, a 1-inch left margin might provide a better appearance. Thus, a 1-inch right margin would be necessary as well.

The bottom-page margin should be the same size as the side margins. If your company's letterhead includes any printed matter at the bottom, the margin should be calculated from the top edge of the printed material rather than from the bottom edge of the page.

Spacing for business letters is invariably single. Double spacing or triple spacing is rare, although some modified spacing can be used for extremely short letters or as a form of emphasis for limited material. Use spacing as a means for centering a one-page letter on the page, to avoid a distorted appearance.

k. Continuation page heading:

When letters exceed a page, continuation pages should contain three forms of information: (1) the full name of the person to whom the letter is addressed, (2) the date of the letter, and (3) the page number. These headings can be set up in several ways; however, the format should conform to the margin formats used throughout the letter. For block style and modified block style (the most common formats), set up the continuation page headings on three lines, either on the far left or far right of the page.

Block style continuation line:
Mr. Robert Smith
October 9, 1997
Page Two

If the letter is using other than a block style, the headings can be set up in a modified form. The name may be aligned with the left margin, page number in the middle, and the date on the right.

Modified continuation line:

Mr. Robert Smith   -2-   October 9, 1997

Continuation headings sometimes repeat reference lines from the first page. This is not usual practice. However, if you write more than one letter to the same person on the same date, you may distinguish them from each other with this additional line on continuation pages.

I. Enclosures:

If the letter is accompanied with enclosures, those should be identified beneath the signature block at the end of the letter. Several acceptable formats are used to indicate enclosures.

- *One item is enclosed.* Spell out the full word or provide an abbreviation beneath the signature block.

Examples:
Enclosure
Enc.

- *More than one item is enclosed.* In this case, indicate the number of enclosures only or list them with a brief description.

Examples:
Enclosures (3)

Enc. (3)

Enclosures:
 (1) Budget report
 (2) Projection worksheet
 (3) Revision recommendations

• *Material is sent separately and is of interest to the reader.* In this instance, indicate that related materials were mailed separately.

Example:
Enclosures:
    (1) Projection worksheet
    (2) Revision recommendations
Sent separately:
    (3) Budget report

m. Carbon copy notation:

Letters are often sent to people other than the person to whom the letter is addressed. The list of those copied is often more important than the contents of the letter, since you are showing the letter's recipient the names of others who will also receive the same letter. For example, when complaining about poor service at a store, you might write to the store's manager and send a copy to the vice president of marketing at the headquarters office.

The term *carbon copy* is held over from the days when all letters were typed and before photocopy machines and word processors were in common use. A file copy as well as several carbon copies were created on a typewriter using carbon paper. Today, of course, this method is rarely used. The "cc." notation is still in use but is often referred to as a "courtesy copy."

The indication "cc." is placed below the signature block and, if applicable, below the enclosure notation. Following the "cc." the name or names of all people receiving copies are listed. The indication may be given in several ways.

Examples:
cc
cc.
copy to (one copied only)
copies to (several people copied)

Following the notation ("cc." is most common), list the name or names of all others receiving copies. If the recipient of the letter and the cc. list are all within the same organization, their titles are not necessary. However, titles should always be included if the cc. list goes to people in different companies.

Example:
> cc. Fred J. Green, President, Markets Co.
> Andrea Smyth, Vice-President, Markets Co.
> Susan Howard, Manager, Markets Co. Store 113

Sometimes you will want to send a copy of a letter to someone but not include that person's name on the cc. list. In that case, type or write the person's name on his or her copy only, under the notation *bcc.* ("blind carbon copy").

Example:
> bcc: Mike Bandor, Customer Service, Markets Co.

n. Postscript:

A postscript is an afterthought placed at the very end of the letter. In some applications, a postscript is used intentionally to emphasize a key point or, in sales letters, to place the actual closing. The notation should be limited to one or two lines, following the indication, P.S.

Examples:
> P.S. Please call by Friday, as I will be out of town all of
>   next week.
> P.S. If you act before January 10, your first year's
>   membership fee will be waived.

5.   Set high standards for correct spelling.

All letters leaving the office under your name should be checked and rechecked for spelling. With spell-checker systems in virtually all word processing systems, this is normally a simple procedure but one that should be executed without fail. Be sure to pay special attention to the correct spelling of names, especially the name of the person to whom the letter is addressed.

See also: SAMPLE FORMS SECTION

*   *   *

Lists

Business applications for lists are virtually endless. Lists are used in reports, budgets, memos and letters, and project schedules.

1. Employ parallel structure in lists.

A list should always be structured so that every item has the same grammatical format. The most preferable format is to begin with a verb. If a list is constructed with full items consisting of full sentences or phrases only, all items on the list should follow that same format. Strive for lists beginning with verbs and containing full sentences.

Improperly constructed list:
1. Define responsibilities for the committee.
2. Task and deadline definitions.
3. Progress review (weekly).
4. Compile and merge information.
5. Final report.

Properly constructed list:
1. Define responsibilities for the committee.
2. Assign tasks and deadlines.
3. Review progress every week.
4. Compile and merge information.
5. Prepare the final report.

2. Observe the rules for lists within paragraphs.

Some lists come at the end of a paragraph; others are contained within a paragraph. If the list is short, it should be contained without any special indentation. This is called an enclosed list.

An enclosed list:

> Our committee will (1) define responsibilities, (2) assign tasks and deadlines, (3) review progress every week, (4) compile and merge the information, and (5) prepare the final report.

An alternative format is to indent the list. This *displayed list* has the advantage of drawing attention to it and providing emphasis at the same time. It is the right choice for longer lists and lists with sublists.

Displayed list:

> Our committee will:
> (1) define responsibilities
> (2) assign tasks and deadlines
> (3) review progress every week
> (4) compile and merge the information
> (5) prepare the final report

Leeway is allowed for rules of punctuation in displayed lists. The only absolute rule is consistency. Note the following differences between the enclosed list and the displayed list in the previous examples:

- The displayed list is broken off from the paragraph by a colon after the word *will.*
- The short action statements all begin with a verb but, because they are not full sentences, are not ended with periods. If the items were full sentences, ending each item with a period would be appropriate but not necessary.
- The word *and* is dropped before the last list item in the displayed form.

3. Designate list items consistently.

You may use numbers, letters, dashes, or bullets to set off the items on a list. None of these methods has special value over the other. Consistent selection of list numbering is recommended when more than one list appears in the same document.

You may determine a series of list rules for your own use. Following are examples of such rules:

- Use numbers as the first level for lists, with letters for sublists.
- Use numbers to identify priorities or sequences.
- Use bullets or dashes for lists in which all steps have equal importance or when the order is not important.

4. Apply uniform treatment throughout the list.

The only hard and fast rule for lists is to be consistent, although there are general guidelines.

a. Capitalization:

Capitalize the first word of every item in an enclosed list (or a displayed list) when all items are complete sentences. Do not capitalize the items in an enclosed list when they are not complete sentences. The first word for each item in a displayed list can be lowercase or capitalized if the item is not a complete sentence.

b. Parentheses:

Enclose the identifying number of list items in parentheses for all enclosed lists. For displayed lists, parentheses can be used, but the preferred method is not to use parentheses and to insert a period after the number or letter.

Enclosed list:
> The steps are (1) prepare the initial report, (2) submit it for review, and (3) redraft.

Displayed list with parentheses:
> (1) Prepare the initial report.
> (2) Submit it for review.
> (3) Redraft the report.

Preferred form for displayed list:

1. Prepare the initial report.
2. Submit it for review.
3. Redraft the report.

c. Colons:

Do not use a colon to introduce an enclosed list when it is within a continuing sentence. In most instances of enclosed lists, list items follow verbs or prepositions.

Enclosed lists:

Our marketing plan identifies (a) markets, (b) competitive forces, (c) projected revenues, and (d) profits.

Our marketing plan is designed to (a) define markets, (b) identify competitive forces, (c) project revenues, and (d) estimate profits.

Colons are used to introduce displayed lists.

Displayed list:

Our marketing plan has four goals:
1. Define markets.
2. Identify competitive forces.
3. Project revenues.
4. Estimate profits.

d. Periods:

End each item in a displayed list with a period when it is a complete sentence. Some lists set up in displayed form are, in fact, one sentence; that is, each item is part of a continuing sentence. In this case, each item concludes with a comma, and a period is placed at the end of the final item. This technique should be used only for short lists. Note that items are not capitalized in this application, and the word *and* is used in the next-to-last item. Effectively, this is an example of a displayed list using the rules of an enclosed list.

Example:
We will implement our plans with
1. complete market analysis,
2. analysis of customer patterns, and
3. product introduction.

5.   Distinguish between lists and sublists.

When a list has sublists, distinguish them by different numbering and lettering systems. Use the displayed list format when sublists are needed. The usual convention is to use numbers for the main list and lowercase letters for the sublist.

A list with sublists:
1. Prepare the budget worksheets:
   a. Format
   b. Responsibility
   c. Uniformity
2. Complete the worksheets:
   a. Centralized control
   b. Departmental input
   c. Deadlines
3. Review preliminary work:
   a. Task force membership
   b. Meeting schedule
   c. Authority for changes

Distinguish between the list and sublist within a report or memo and the outline, which stands alone and is intended to present a course of action, priorities, or steps in a process. The outline is a detailed list complete with sublists (possibly on more than one level).

When a list becomes too complex to use within the body of another document, set it aside and refer to it as an attachment. That helps avoid overly long memos and letters. It enables the writer to use the space to describe key points rather than presenting too much detail. A list should be short enough to include within the body of another document, without distracting the reader.

See also: Outlining; Parallelism

*   *   *

Manuscripts

The manuscript is a semifinal draft of a document being prepared for a final version. Businesspeople deal with manuscripts of especially long reports, brochures, or books produced within an organization or association. Final copy is prepared from the manuscript in bound form, with properly typeset narratives, photographs, and graphics, and bound in adequate numbers for distribution.

Manuscript is derived from the original meaning of handwritten script. Today it usually refers to a document in hard copy or on disk, being made ready for production and distribution.

1. Use the proper paper for editing.

Always use plain white paper, $8\frac{1}{2}$ by 11 inches, for preparation of a manuscript. Never use erasable or onionskin bond paper. Do not submit carbon copies for proofreading. If you do a photocopy, ensure that the quality is adequate so that an editor can read the text without difficulty.

2. Follow guidelines for text preparation.

If you are provided with manuscript guidelines, read them thoroughly and follow all directions.

a. Spacing:

Manuscripts should always be double-spaced (some sources will require triple-spaced manuscripts), to provide adequate room for making corrections.

b. Numbering:

Pages should be numbered consecutively throughout the manuscript, beginning with page 1. This allows one or more editors to refer to the manuscript page for indicating corrections.

c. Page headings:

Page headings provide important information. Most word processing systems enable you to preset page headings automatically as *headers*. The header should contain enough information to identify the topic of the entire manuscript and the source, or author. A popular format is to include the title and author at the left and the page number at the right top of each page.

Example:

Marketing Plan   Page 62
John Green

d. Ancillary material:

When graphics, tables, and photographs are part of the manuscript, clearly label each one, and indicate its placement in the final version. Cover a camera-ready graphic with a protective sheet of transparent paper and label it. Also place an indication in the text.

Example:

(Insert Photo 3-18 here)

3. Follow indicated standards for corrections and editing.

Make all corrections to your manuscript using the proper editing and proofreading marks. (See Figure E-1.) Each individual working on a manuscript should use a designated color of pencil or pen agreed to in advance. Color coding allows subsequent editors to identify the source of corrections and to determine whether changes are mandatory or only suggestions.

Before editing make sure that all people involved in the project are agreed on (1) responsibility for editing at each phase,

(2) deadlines and methods, and (3) authority for changes and final approval.

4.   Properly cross-reference the manuscript.

Manuscripts should be prepared with thorough cross-references between text and graphics or between text and material in appendixes. Select the cross-reference standards—for example: standards are:

- All charts and graphs are to be numbered by chapter. For example, Chapter 6 will begin illustration cross-reference with the designations *6-1, 6-2,* and *6-3.*
- All tables within the manuscript will be lettered for each chapter. For example, Chapter 6 will begin table cross-reference with the designations *6-A, 6-B,* and *6-C.*
- All photographs within the manuscript will be numbered with roman numerals for each chapter. For example, Chapter 6 will begin photograph cross-references with the designations *6-I, 6-II,* and *6-III.*

5.   Adhere to all publication company standards and practices.

Some business reports and other documents are published within the organization or by an outside publisher. Adhere to all publisher standards in the preparation of manuscripts and other materials.

Publishers expect to receive the original of the manuscript and possibly one photocopy (some publishers ask for two copies). In addition, you will probably be asked to supply the manuscript on diskette. Be sure to ascertain (1) the diskette type desired, (2) the format or program, and (3) the labeling desired by the publisher.

Also determine and agree on deadlines for submission. Does the publisher want the entire manuscript, or are you expected to submit chapters or sections as they are completed? Ask for detailed guidelines from the publisher. Read them thoroughly and follow all instructions. Establish a primary and secondary contact person within the organization for editing and for production (preparation and editing of the manuscript and actual publication).

See also: Charts and Graphs; Citations; Editing and Proofreading; Footnotes; Photographs; Tables of Contents

*   *   *

Mathematical Symbols

How mathematical symbols are styled in business correspondence and reports varies based on the topic, type of industry and company, and nature of the report. In highly technical applications, the individual preparing reports will have available the specialized software and equipment for using mathematical notation. For any other application, the guidelines that follow should be applied.

1. Determine placement of mathematical expressions.

Only very simple mathematical expressions should run in with the text. For longer, more complex expressions, space should be left both above and below the expression, and it should be indented.

Example of a poorly placed expression:
Correct application of the formula $[F + 1] + [Y3]^2 = C$ is to be confined to the primary tests.

Example of a clarified expression:
Primary testing is the only proper application of this formula:

$$[F + 1] + [Y3]^2 = C$$

Also, if the word processing system you use allows, it is preferable to italicize the variables but not the symbols or numbers.

When special symbols exceed a single line of text, the top and bottom spacing should be measured from the edges of those symbols. Some statistical and technical equations involve extended bracketing and the use of symbols exceeding one line in size.

2.   Be consistent in format.

The format selected for mathematical notation should be used consistently throughout the report or other document. The choices for methods vary widely, so selection of a clear and concise style for expression is an important step in communication and style.

Within scaled formula expressions, consistency of scale and system is essential. Do not, for example, alternate between meters and yards for length-related expressions. Do not alter expressions between numbering systems or use symbolic representation inconsistently. For reports containing a large number of mathematical expressions, help the reader by providing a brief summary of symbols used and their definitions, including mathematical value when applicable.

3.   Be aware of conventional accounting and financial notation guidelines.

The most common form of mathematical notation in business involves finance: accounting reports as well as reports concerning financial results prepared by nonaccounting departments. For reporting dollars and cents, the following guidelines should be observed:

- Align all dollar amounts on the decimal point.

Example:

$5,230.43
13.99
113.67

- Use dollar signs only for the first value in a column and for the grand total. Do not use the cents symbol (¢) in financial reports. The dollar sign should always be aligned on the same location, and the totaling rule extends to under the dollar sign.

Example:

$$\begin{array}{r} \$5,230.43 \\ 13.99 \\ \underline{113.67} \\ \$5,358.09 \end{array}$$

- When financial values appear in text, (1) spell out round dollar amounts below $100, (2) use numerals for all amounts that contain both dollars and cents, and (3) use numerals for all values included in narratives of $100 or more.

Examples:

The unit price is seven dollars.
The product price is below the ten-dollar level.
The price is $7.03 per unit.
The product costs $9.95 at the retail level.
Each store nets about $200.00 per day.
The average store nets $205.13 per day.
The candy bar is forty-nine cents.

- Dollar and cent values include commas and decimal points. Include decimal points for *all* dollar values, even when no cents are included. Always follow the decimal point with two digits, even if both are zero. Commas are inserted every three spaces to make the values easier to read.

Incorrect expressions:

$5230.
$42.6

Correct expressions:

$5,230.00
$ 42.60

4. Financial values expressed in text should be limited to a discussion of significance.

Do not merely repeat the information shown in a table. Consider the following examples, both based on the table shown with the example.

Table appearing with text:

Table 1

Salaries	$35,669.90
Office expenses	$47,800.42
Selling expenses	37,593.20
Total	$121,063.52

Poor narrative:

Salaries this period were $35,669.90. Office expenses were $47,800.42. Selling expenses were $37,593.20. The total of all expenses for the period was $121,063.52.

Preferred narrative style:

Table 1 demonstrates the relationship of the three major expense groupings. Overall expenses have not changed since the previous quarter. However, office expenses have declined, while selling expenses have risen because of improved internal budget controls and higher sales activity.

The first example repeats what the table already shows, providing the reader with no new information and presenting a hard-to-read summary. The second example refers to the table and offers insights on the significance of what the table shows.

The second example is by far more informative, and more interesting too.

5. Do not punctuate mathematical notation.

Nonfinancial expressions provided in narrative are not punc-
tuated. When an equation is referred to, no comma or colon is
provided at the end of the narrative break.

> *Example:*
> The formula for this is
>
> $$(x + y) + (x + z) = C$$

6. Break multiline expressions at a sign of operation or at the equals sign.

When expressions exceed one line, break the expression at a sign
of operation or at the equals sign. (Signs of operation include
instructions to add, subtract, multiply, or divide.) Do not break
the line in the middle of a grouping enclosed by parentheses.

> *Incorrect break:*
> $$(x + y) + (x$$
> $$+ z) + [rate/12] = P$$
>
> *Correct break:*
> $$(x + y) + (x + z) +$$
> $$(rate/12) = P$$

When an expression exceeds one line, avoid expressing two segments on different pages. If an expression begins at the bottom
of a page, skip extra spaces and place the entire expression on
the following page.

7. Coordinate mathematical notation with explanations.

Some forms of mathematical expression are accompanied with
narrative explanation. Two methods are recommended; the

choice depends on the audience and the intent of the formula being explained.

Narrative with steps indented:

The steps to follow in computing monthly calculations of principal and interest are (1) multiply the previous balance by the annual rate to arrive at the annual interest amount:

$$\$37,950.20 \times 10.00\% = \$3,795.02$$

(2) divide the answer by 12 (months) to arrive at this month's interest total:

$$\$3,795.02/12 = \$316.25$$

(3) subtract the interest amount from this month's total payment to arrive at the principal amount:

$$\$325.00 - \$316.25 = \$8.75$$

and (4) subtract the principal amount from the previous balance to arrive at the new balance forward:

$$\$37,950.20 - \$8.75 = \$37,941.45$$

Narrative with steps to the side:

The steps to follow in computing monthly calculations of principal and interest are:

(1) multiply the previous balance by the annual rate to arrive at the annual interest amount.

$$\begin{array}{r} \$37,950.20 \\ \times \quad\quad .10 \\ \hline \$3,795.02 \end{array}$$

(2) divide the answer by 12 (months) to arrive at this month's interest total.

$$\frac{\$3,795.02}{12}$$

$$\underline{\$316.25}$$

(3) subtract the interest amount from this month's total payment to arrive at the principal amount.	$325.00 −316.25	$ 8.75
(4) subtract the principal amount from the previous balance to arrive at the new balance forward	$37,950.20 − 8.75	$37,941.45

See also: DECIMALS, FRACTIONS, AND PERCENTAGES

*   *   *

MEMOS

The office memo is a widely used and popular way to communicate informally. The memo is a letter written to someone else within the company. Thus, the longer title, "interoffice memorandum," is often used. Some memos are structured carefully, serving as internal reports. Others are less structured, taking the form of a letter or even a brief personal note. Memos can be written from one person or department to another, or issued for distribution to a wider audience, including every employee of the company in many cases.

The principles and guidelines for writing letters apply equally to memos. But because they are internal documents, they do not need to conform as strictly to formatting rules. Good writing, whether in letters or memos, follows the same four guiding principles:

1. Place critical information first.
2. Avoid complex or technical language.
3. Refer to attachments or other reports for details.
4. Remember the audience for the memo.

Finally, distinguish between memos and internal reports. A memo is intended as correspondence and should be brief. You may want to write a cover memo for the longer attachment that serves as a report. The memo should highlight key conclusions, ask for a response, or draw the reader's attention to a section or page of particular interest.

1. Follow formatting guidelines.

The format for the internal memo is vastly different from that of the letter in several ways:

a. Addresses are not provided.

Because the memo is written to an individual or department within the organization, the writer usually needs to indicate only the name. In some cases, a department or separate building address, or a floor or room will be needed as well.

b. The sender's name is placed at the top of the first page.

The memo is not signed, although the sender may initial above his or her typed name. The entire document is usually typed without any written notation whatsoever. Use of the titles *Mr.,* *Mrs.,* or *Ms.* are not normally included on memos.

c. The memo requires no closing statement, such as "sincerely" or "cordially," because there is no signature.

d. The headings of the memo are *Date, To, From,* and *Subject* or variations of these.

Each of these headings is followed by a colon. The information expressed in the heading *Subject* is often underlined for emphasis.

Memo heading:
   Date: February 16, 1997
   To: Bob Robbins
   From: Sarah Thomas
   Subject: *Weekly staff meeting*

e. There are no salutations.

After the heading classifications, the body of the memo begins at once.

2. Include enclosures, copies, and postscripts according to proper guidelines.

At the end of the memo, appropriate notations are made for any attachments. If copies are sent to anyone other than the person named at the top of the memo, the recipients should be listed at the end after the notation *cc*. Postscripts are rarer in memos than they are in letters but can be included at the end. All enclosure, copy, and postscript rules should be followed along the same guidelines as those described in the Letters section.

3. The guidelines for page headings and numbering are the same as for letters.

Number pages beyond a single page using the same guidelines as those provided in the Letters section. The individual to whom the memo is sent, the date, and the page number should be listed on every page of the memo.

4. Break up lengthy sections.

In memos longer than one page, break up the discussion.

a. Subheads:

The most appropriate way to break up a discussion is to use subheads. A topic exceeding one page probably can be broken down into several smaller topics. Subheadings make it easier for the reader to skim through the memo, grasp the scope of the discussion, and seek out points of greatest interest.

b. Outline:

Memos can be broken down and organized in outline form. One method for explaining a complex topic is to design the overall outline headings and then fill in each one as the memo develops. This is an organizational tool for the writer and also serves as a guide to the reader. Outlines are recommended for exceptionally long memos.

c. Summary:

Consider summarizing the major points or conclusions at the front of the memo. The first page then serves as an overview, with the remainder of the memo supporting those major points. The reader can thus see from the first page the extent and scope of the memo. Rather than needing to read through the entire document, the reader can go to the points of greatest interest. When using this technique for long memos, cross-reference the summary section to each section of the memo by numbering the major points and using the corresponding number for each subhead.

See also: LETTERS; SAMPLE FORMS SECTION

*   *   *

NUMERALS AND NUMBERING

Numerals are used extensively in reports, memos, and manuals. Outline form uses several different forms of numerals to mark levels of topics.

1. Express numerals in text as effectively as possible.

Numerical expression is so common in business that it is hardly possible to write any business communication without reference to some form of count or value. The measurement of success is invariably dollars and cents; the measure of performance is quantity. As a result, style guidelines for expressing numerals in text are of critical importance.

a. Percentages, decimals, and fractions:

1. Use numbers combined with the word *percent* spelled out   to express a percentage in text, regardless of the numerical value.

> *Incorrect expressions:*
>> Net profit this year was seven %.
>> Approximately 85% of customers return.
>
> *Correct expressions:*
>> Net profit this year was 7 percent.
>> Approximately 85 percent of customers return

2. Express decimals in numerical form,   regardless of size. Do not include zeros to the far right except when discussing dollars and cents. For values below 1, include a single zero to the left of the decimal point.

> *Incorrect expressions:*
>> The failure rate was 1.530 per 1,000 units.
>> Variance of .45 in. is within acceptable range.
>
> *Correct expressions:*
>> The failure rate was 1.53 per 1,000 units.
>> Variance of 0.45 in. is within acceptable range.

3. Fractions should be expressed with numerals when they are large or complex; they may be spelled out   if each side of the fraction contains a value of a single word.

> *Incorrect expressions:*
>> Only twenty-one three-hundred sixty-fifths of those
>> surveyed responded.

About $\frac{4}{5}$ths of our employees attended some college.

Correct expressions:
Only $2\frac{1}{365}$ths of those surveyed responded.
About four-fifths of our employees attended some college.

b.   Combining whole numbers and fractions:

Whenever a value includes both whole numbers and fractions, the entire value is expressed numerically, regardless of value.

Incorrect expressions:
The size is thirteen and $\frac{3}{5}$ for that project.
We worked only three and $\frac{1}{2}$ days last week.

Correct expressions:
The size is $13\frac{3}{5}$ for that project.
We worked only 3 and $\frac{1}{2}$ days last week.

c.   Plural numbers:

When values are expressed in numerals, a plural is formed by adding an *s* without any punctuation.

Examples:
the 1990s
temperatures in the 80s

Plurals for spelled-out values are made by adding *s* to the word, with the following exception: numerals divisible by 10 are made plural by deleting the *y* and adding *-ies.*

Singular	*Plural*
twenty	twenties
thirty	thirties
forty	forties
fifty	fifties
sixty	sixties
seventy	seventies
eighty	eighties
ninety	nineties

d. Use of commas:

Commas are used when numerical values are spelled out and that value exceeds one thousand. Use commas to separate values in groups of three.

Examples:
1,000
13,533
426,385

e. Dates:

Dates in text are always combinations of fully spelled out months or days of the week, with numerical values to express dates and years.

Incorrect expressions:
Mon, Jun. 13
February fourteenth, 1997
the first Mon. in 8.

Correct expressions:
Monday, June 13
February 14, 1997
the first Monday in August

In memos and other informal correspondence and in accounting and financial reports, dates are referred to in abbreviated form.

Acceptable date formats:
6/26/97   Aug. 27, 1996

f. Numerals or words:

As a general guideline, write out whole numbers of ten or lower; use numerals for whole numbers above ten.

When discussing exceptionally large values (millions, for example), use numerals even for amounts below ten; and spell out the value word rather than including a large number of zeros. When the large numbers are dollar amounts, include dollar signs rather than spelling out the word *dollars*.

Undesirable style:
more than seven million dollars
population growth of 14,000,000

Preferred style:
more than $7 million
population growth of 14 million

g. Numbers beginning sentences:

Always spell out numbers beginning sentences.

Incorrect expressions:
14 employees are in the department.
$20 is the balance of the fund.

Correct expressions:
Fourteen employees are in the department.
Twenty dollars is the balance of the fund.

If the number is especially large, avoid beginning a sentence with the value.

Large number at beginning of sentence:
Four thousand twenty-seven customers came through the doors on opening day.

Preferred style:
On opening day, 4,027 customers came through the doors.

h. Consistency:

When several numbers occur within the same sentence, be consistent. Do not change the form just to conform to the general rules of expression.

Incorrect expression:

> The first shift reported three defects, the second shift 14, and the third shift only two.

Preferred expressions:

> The first shift reported three defects, the second shift fourteen, and the third shift only two.
> The first shift reported 3 defects, the second shift 14, and the third shift only 2.

Avoid statements mixing value expressions even for dissimilar values.

Mixed value expression:

> The report showed that 14 stores reported seven incidents of theft, while the remaining six stores reported an average of 20 incidents.

Preferred style:

> The report showed that 14 stores reported 7 incidents of theft, while the remaining 6 stores reported an average of 20 incidents.

2. Use numerical expressions to clarify a point.

The ratio is an effective tool for communication. Use this abbreviated expression to clarify what would otherwise be a difficult-to-explain series of numbers.

Unclear statement:

> Although the company's profits were more than $70 million, direct costs accounted for $63 million in the same period.

Example of clarifying ratio statement:

> After direct costs, the company retained only one dollar out of every ten dollars of sales.

3.   Use numbering systems to clarify and distinguish.

Numbers alone or in combination with letters can be used in several ways, depending on the application. When several levels apply, combine uses of numbers of different systems with upper-case and lowercase letters. Levels can also be distinguished with the selection of a period following the number or letter or enclosing the number or letter in parentheses.

Example of multiple levels:
   I. Level one
      A. Level two
         1. Level three
            a. Level four
               (1) Level five
                  (a) Level six

Such breakdowns are commonly used in outline form, where levels may become quite detailed.

A modified form of levels is found in instruction and procedures manuals. Levels of headings are further divided by the use of levels broken up by decimal points.

Decimal system numbering:
   1   Major division
   1.1   First detail level
   1.1.1   Second detail level
   1.1.1.1 Third detail level

Using this system, new information can be inserted in subsequent modifications or additions to a manual, without having to renumber the existing references. Some divisions can have very large breakdowns within each section, while other divisions will not necessarily contain the same volume of information.

See also: DECIMALS, FRACTIONS, AND PERCENTAGES; FINANCIAL REPORTS; MATHEMATICAL SYMBOLS

*   *   *

ORGANIZATION CHARTS

Organizations use graphic representations to demonstrate the chain of command in the company. The organization chart shows the reporting chain, usually with the highest rank on the top and the lowest on the bottom.

1. Exclude stockholders and directors.

The organization chart normally begins with the chief executive officer (CEO) or the president at the top. Although stockholders and a board of directors are actually higher in rank than this position, they are not usually included on the graphic. The organization chart is normally limited to the internal organization.

2. Limit the amount of detail.

Because organizations may have a complex reporting system, the organization chart should be limited in scope. Except in relatively small companies, not everyone's position can be included. Cut off the detail at senior or middle management positions, depending on the number of posts to be included. Remember the purpose of the organization chart: to demonstrate the broad reporting perspective of the company, not to include every detail.

3. Connect with solid lines only.

As a general rule, each position should be connected to those above and below with a solid line. Arrows are not used, since the reporting chain is already obvious. Positions equal in rank should be on the same vertical line.

Figure O-1 shows a simplified organization chart outline. In this example, there are four levels in the chain of command. On the top is the president or CEO, followed by two divisional or vice-presidential lines. On the far left, the second-level position has three departments reporting, and one of those has an

Figure O-1. Simplified Format for Organization Chart

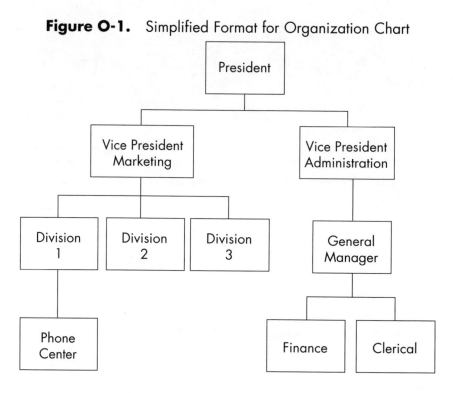

additional level reporting. The far-right vice president has one level, which in turn has two additional reporting levels.

This format demonstrates how various types of reporting can be facilitated on the organization chart. Note that at each level, the boxes representing departments or divisions are on the same line to avoid confusion about rank or relative influence within the company.

A solid line should be used between all levels to indicate a clear line of the chain of command. Some organization charts connect boxes with a broken line, which often indicates that the chain of command is unclear at that point. When an executive hires a special assistant, for example, that individual reports directly and may not fit within the traditional chain of command. One business observer, Robert Townsend, wrote in his book, *Further Up the Organization,* that "the traditional organization chart has one dead giveaway. Any dotted line indicates a trouble-maker and/or a serious troubled relationship." This statement might seem humorous, but there is enough truth in it to merit attention. If the organization chart cannot be constructed with a clearly understood chain of command, there is probably a serious reporting problem. And that is the point of going through the effort to construct an organization chart. It forces definition.

4. Include titles but not names.

When organization charts are published in orientation manuals, displays, annual reports, and other documents going outside the company, the title of each position should be included but actual names should be left out. When organization charts are for internal distribution, names should be given along with each title, so that employees know not only the reporting chain but the people at each executive and management level.

See also: Flowcharts

*   *   *

Outlining

The outline is a useful device for organizing thoughts prior to writing reports, memos, letters, and other documents. Outlines should be compiled from notes or from a large body of information, so that the sequence of presentation can be decided prior to beginning the writing task. The sequence of information is one of the most important factors in style, since clarity of expression is determined by the way that information is presented.

1. Follow the guidelines for labeling outline levels.

Use numbers and/or letters consistently to identify the different levels of an outline. A *level* is a distinct topic or subtopic. For example, the first level may be one of six major points made in the outline. Within each of the six major categories, a number of secondary points are made; and within each of those, several third-level points are made.

Example:

   I. Roman numerals distinguish level 1
      1. Align roman numerals on the decimal
      2. Indent second-level points
  II. A limited number of major topics is presented
      1. Follow the same numbering system throughout
      2. Note the similarity of numbering at the second level
         (a) Numbering is the same
         (b) Indentation is the same
         (c) Each level, including level 3, has a distinct numbering distinction

2. Limit the number of outline levels.

Outlines can become confusing if too many levels are used. Strive for a limited number of sublevels. Major points are the beginning for organizing your outline. Start by listing the major points; then identify two to five second-level topics. Within those, add detail as needed at a third level. Going beyond a third level might be unnecessary except in extremely lengthy and detailed outlines. Be aware that when you reach beyond fourth and fifth levels of detail, readers begin to lose their perspective about what the outline conveys. Avoid excessive detail at this phase. Always remember what the outline is intended to achieve.

3. Use outlines for thought organization.

Outlining is an excellent way to organize a complex topic into logical breakdowns. When preparing a report or even an especially long letter or memo, use outline form to prioritize your message. Outlines can help you to identify the proper sequence of teaching blocks. Without using the outline form, information might be disorganized, out of order, and ineffective.

4.   Use outlines for organizing presentations.

Outlines are effective tools for organizing a presentation in several formats.

a.   Speeches:

When you are asked to give a speech on a topic you understand well, reading from exact notes is stilted and unfamiliar. Outline form provides you with a train of thought, while still allowing an informal style. The outline allows you to interact with the audience without losing a train of thought in the middle of the speech.

b.   Meetings:

Outlines for presentations made in meetings provide the same benefits as they do in speeches. You should be intimately familiar with the topic and with the material to be presented. Using outlines ensures that you will present material in the proper order, you will not overlook important points, and you will get through all of the material even if you are interrupted with questions or comments.

c.   Reports:

When preparing reports for distribution, start with an outline to prioritize the presentation of data. The outline may later serve as a Table of Contents for cross-reference to each section, an idea of notable value in reports exceeding a few pages in length. The longer the report is, the more important it is to provide the reader with an outline.

5.   Employ parallel structure in outlines.

When presenting information in outline form, be sure that each statement at each level follows consistent parallel structure. If the outline contains action statements (a preferred and recommended format), all statements should be presented in that way.

Inconsistent structure:

I. Presentation of information.
  1. Identify needed data.
  2. Preliminary presentation.
  3. Review and modify.
  4. Make final presentation.

Action statements in parallel form:

I. Present information.
  1. Identify needed data.
  2. Present information (preliminary).
  3. Review and modify presentation.
  4. Present information (final).

Note the action orientation of the second example compared to the inconsistent and passive tone in the first example. Parallel structure is easier to read and gives others a clearer idea of the intention behind the outline.

See also: LISTS; PARALLELISM

*   *   *

PARAGRAPHS

A paragraph is a group of sentences consistent in thought or theme. A break between paragraphs signals a new idea or thought, or expansion on the previous material. The beginning sentence of the paragraph is transitional (from previous material) or forms the topic of the new paragraph. As the topic is introduced, the idea is developed in the remainder of the paragraph.

1. Provide a topic sentence.

The topic sentence usually appears at the beginning of the paragraph, although it may appear in the middle on occasion, especially when the paragraph begins with the transition. Ideally, the paragraph's topic and transition are merged together in one sentence, creating the most efficient and readable paragraph.

2.   Use transitions between paragraphs to ensure continuity of thought.

Generally each paragraph is dedicated to a single idea or series of ideas; the break between paragraphs represents a move from one idea to another or an expansion of the thought. Transitions are bridges between paragraphs and are usually the first sentence in a new paragraph. The transition should also serve as the new topic sentence.

> *Paragraphs with transitions:*
>
> We are announcing our new product this week. After more than two years of research and testing, we believe that this improved product will be less expensive, more efficient, and safer than any other product for similar use on the market today.
>
> The attached test results dramatically illustrate the point. Never before has a product offering these combined benefits been offered at a lower price than the range of products it is replacing. We are confident that our customers will agree with our conclusions once they have tried the product.

In the first paragraph, the lead sentence establishes the subject and is the topic sentence. In the second paragraph, the first sentence serves two purposes: it is the topic sentence and serves as a transition from the material introduced in the previous paragraph, and the discussion that follows.

3.   Vary paragraph length.

Although length should be dictated by the subject matter, a series of exceptionally long paragraphs is difficult to digest, and a series of paragraphs too short in length is distracting and disjointed. Paragraph length should be varied between two and seven sentences, as a general rule. A single topic will rarely require more length than this. However, when paragraphs do exceed this length, they can be broken up with lists or, if quotations are included, indented sections for specialized text. The narrative of reports, memos, letters, and other documents should be visually varied—meaning paragraphs of different lengths—to keep reader interest at a maximum.

By definition, a paragraph contains more than one sentence. However, a one-sentence paragraph can be a dramatic form of emphasis if used very selectively. Such a device may be obvious or very subtle.

A dramatic one-sentence paragraph:

This week's seminar includes an exceptionally busy program and more than the usual number of speakers. Accordingly, scheduling is going to be more difficult than possible, especially if the audience has a large number of questions.

Do not go over your allotted time.

There are no exceptions to this rule. If you do not stop on time, you will be interrupted and the next speaker brought forward. So keep an eye on the clock.

The one-sentence paragraph in this example, "Do not go over your allotted time," adds a lot of emphasis. It conveys the idea clearly that no exceptions will be tolerated.

A subtle one-sentence paragraph:

Changes in last year's budgetary process were criticized at first as being too cumbersome for staff. However, once the process began, we discovered that the new procedures took no more time than before.

The most dramatic result of the new procedures has been a much improved budget, with fewer unexplained variances and a better cost tracking system.

With the satisfying results in mind, we propose to export these procedures to the divisional level, where we still have big problems. We think that the procedure can work on all levels and would ask, at the very least, that we try it out at one division to see whether positive changes result.

The transitions between these three paragraphs work because

the original idea is introduced and explained (paragraph 1); the major benefit is summarized in the one-sentence paragraph (paragraph 2); and a recommendation for further action is provided (paragraph 3). Because of the smoothness in the transition, the single-sentence paragraph works well and adds subtle emphasis.

4. Use a consistent point of view to achieve unity in the paragraph (and throughout the rest of the narrative).

Point of view is the voice in which the document is expressed. Most business writing employs various voices, depending on the nature of the document.

Inconsistent voice:

We intend to continue monitoring the procedures in this department. I will be involved in this directly, as it is my responsibility to ensure successful completion and submission of the report each week. We will keep you informed.

Improved voice:

I intend to continue monitoring the procedures directly. I am responsible for ensuring successful completion and submission of the report each week. I will keep you informed.

5. Organize paragraphs logically.

Always assume that a reader is unfamiliar with your material, so any explanatory matter should precede concluding remarks or suggestions. If background data are especially long, refer to them in the main body of the report, and include background discussions as an attachment.

If the narrative is exceptionally long, organize the writing and arrangement of paragraphs by first constructing an outline. Arrange important points in logical sequence, remembering to build the discussion on a solid foundation, establishing a case as you proceed.

As a method of emphasis or dramatic expression, a particularly interesting point can be placed at the beginning of a lengthy narrative, followed by background and supporting information. This makes an otherwise dreary discussion more interesting than the sequential discussion of a complicated issue. This technique, referred to as a *hook,* is used in some styles of writing, particularly in trade magazines. There may be applications in business writing as well, especially in letters.

> *A hook in paragraph arrangement:*
> We can reduce our budget by 20 percent this year just by adding a single step in the existing procedures: an idea that will cost nothing but will yield returns over many, many years.

This paragraph is meant to entice the reader into wanting to read more. Of course, it should be followed with supportable proof of the claim. A decision maker reading this paragraph would expect to see data and to be convinced that nothing will be lost by taking the suggestion alluded to.

6.   Indenting decisions depend on the nature of the document and the style of expression.

In the traditional style, the first line of each paragraph is indented five spaces. No extra space is left between paragraphs. An alternative method is not to indent the first line of each paragraph but to leave one full space between each paragraph.

> *Indented paragraphs:*
> Speakers at orientation seminars usually give long, boring speeches that put their audience to sleep. I intend to give a short, boring speech that will not put you to sleep.
> I do have a lot of material to get through, so let's get right to it. If anyone has questions as we proceed, raise your hand and ask as we go along.

> *Unindented paragraphs:*
> The market has not actually changed over the past 50 years, although our product line has changed

dramatically. What does this mean? Is there a limit to the very idea of product development and improvement, and how do we recognize when we're there?

Our marketing department argues that there is not such a limit. They would like to continue devoting a portion of their budget to product research and development, and their arguments are convincing.

The choice of style depends on the rules imposed by the organization, if any. Some companies prefer all letters to conform to one style, typically the unindented block style. If reports and other documents are doubled-spaced as a matter of practice, unindented style is a preferred formatting decision. The style selected for a specific type of document should be used consistently for each version and application.

See also: OUTLINING; SENTENCES

*   *   *

PARALLELISM

Clarity and power of expression are improved by being aware of the need for parallelism in style. When you express a series of ideas in a list, in outline form, or in a table, use parallel construction. This is a method for making similar statements similar in format.

1. Use parallelism for list and outline organization.

Outline form is popular as a method for organizing thoughts, preparing presentations and speeches, and presenting reports or action plans. Use parallel structure on all outlines for clarity and consistency of style.

Unparallel structure:

A. Building parallel thoughts
   1. Identify the list
   2. Listing in sequence
   3. Write out the list
   4. Making the presentation

Parallel structure:

A. Building parallel thoughts
   1. Identify the list
   2. List in sequence
   3. Write out the list
   4. Make the presentation

The second example contains a consistent listing of action statements; the list in the first example is a combination of action ideas and passive statements.

2.   Use parallel forms of parts of speech.

When listing items, write so that the parallel parts of speech are set up in parallel form. This guideline applies to verbs, nouns, and phrases.

Unparallel verbs:

1. Following up
2. Communicate
3. Making changes

Parallel verbs:

1. Following up
2. Communicating
3. Making changes

Unparallel nouns:

1. Accounting department coordination
2. Manager of sales should prepare budget
3. Bob Smith to approve process

Parallel alternative:

1. Accounting manager coordinates

2. Sales manager prepares budget
3. Vice president approves

Unparallel phrases:
1. Problems:
   a. Communicating
   b. Of improving methods
   c. Executive level

Parallel alternative:
1. Problems:
   a. In communication
   b. Of improving methods
   c. At executive level

*   *   *

PARENTHESES AND BRACKETS

Enclosing a group of words within text is one form of emphasis. It also serves other purposes.

1. Use parentheses for asides within text.

The use of parentheses in some situations helps add a conversational tone to narrative. The aside is a thought off the subject by way of added information, a side thought, or necessary explanation that adds to the discussion at hand.

Asides:
The director of sales (who has had over 20 years experience in the field) expressed his opinion without hesitation.
Our sales volume last year (which was below projected levels but exceeded previous records) cannot be used as an indication of the future, due to substantial changes in markets.

> Mr. Martins (who is approachable and open to
> suggestions from subordinates) could be asked to
> consider this recommendation.

In each example, the information enclosed in parentheses is not essential to the meaning of the sentence, but it does have an effect on how the reader will interpret the information. Parentheses can be used effectively without distraction, as long as their use is essential. Like any other style device, excessive use also destroys the impact and intention.

2.   Enclose citations and examples in parentheses.

Parentheses are used to provide documentation of source material and to provide examples within narrative. The intent is to avoid distracting the reader's train of thought while providing essential secondary information.

Citations within text:
> According to Dr. Hamilton (*Budgets on Computer*, 1995, p. 246), zero-base models were three times more likely to be attainable.
> Research in this field (*Business Facts,* Oct. 1997) shows that only a small percentage of such programs are even minimally effective.

In-text examples:
> The primary causes of defects (fatigue, monotony, low morale) are also the most difficult to eliminate.
> There is little we can do to cut further those overhead expenses established by contract (payroll, rents, leases, and interest).

3.   Use parentheses to set aside definitions, abbreviations, and acronyms.

Use parentheses to clarify narrative explanations for definitions and acronyms used in the text. Within a single document, it is necessary to provide this type of clarity only the first time that the definition or acronym arises.

Definitions:
> The contingent liability (a liability that might or might not become an actual liability) is included as a footnote by standard practice.

Abbreviation:
> Our CFO (chief financial officer) has issued the report and is currently distributing it.

Acronym:
> The guidelines issued last month by HUD (Housing and Urban Development) define how we must comply with those regulations.

4. Use parentheses for list distinctions.

Parentheses are used in enclosed lists.

Example:
> Our priorities are to (1) select deadlines, (2) assign work, and (3) complete the report.

5. Use parentheses and brackets for emphasis.

Parentheses and brackets can be used for emphasis; however, overuse will tend to destroy the effect.

Parentheses for emphasis:
> Net profits ($45,769) exceeded the forecast by a significant margin.

Parentheses used excessively:
> Net (after-income taxes) profits ($45,759) exceeded the forecast ($38,000) by a significant margin (20.4%).

6. In contracts, use parentheses for numbers.

In contracts, dollar amounts and other numbers are often both spelled out and given numerically.

Example:
> The consideration of $10,000 (ten thousand dollars) will be paid in full within 20 (twenty) days.

7. Use parentheses and brackets appropriately in mathematical expressions.

Mathematical expressions are dependent on the use of parentheses, brackets, or both.

Example:
$$(x + y) + (r[2 \times P]) = J$$

8. Follow the rules of punctuation for parentheses and brackets.

A brief phrase or word enclosed in brackets or parentheses within a sentence is not usually closed with a period.

Examples:
> The manager (of the division) stood up and objected to the criticism.
> The division manager stood up and objected to the criticism (as he has done at each preceding meeting).

When the enclosed section is itself a sentence, the punctuation belongs inside the parenthesis.

Example:
> The division manager stood up and objected to the criticism. (He has made a practice of objecting at least once in each such meeting.)

If the enclosed material asks a question, the question mark belongs inside the parenthesis.

Example:

> The division manager stood up and objected to the criticism (hasn't he done this at previous meetings?).

Parentheses are used in some cases to indicate either a singular or plural. The *s* at the end of the word, when enclosed in brackets, indicates that there is a choice or that the correct number is not known.

Example:

> The employee(s) preparing the report overlooked several important details.

9.   Use brackets for errors in original quotations being cited verbatim.

Brackets are used in quotations when an error is included in the original quotation in spelling or grammar or when the quotation is confusing as it stands. When within the quotation, such errors should not be corrected. They should be followed with the bracketed word *sic,* advising the reader that the error was part of the quotation and not part of your transcription.

Example:

> According to the report, "Without fail, all members of the staff was [*sic*] part of the volunteer effort."

Brackets used when within a direct quotation imply that the enclosed word or words are not directly part of the actual quotation. This technique is used when, due to the way in which the quotation is being used, it would be awkward to quote directly. For example, consider the following passage found in a quoted source:

Text example:

> These brave young women were unwilling to allow

employers to take advantage of them because of their
sex.

If you want to use this quotation in a paragraph already discussing females and job relations, it might read as:

Application example:
"Women of the 1890s were noteworthy in this
employment rights struggle. The author notes, "[They]
were unwilling to allow employers to take advantage of
them because of their sex."

Because the narrative has already established the subject of discussion, the actual quotation would be awkward. By using brackets, the context of the quotation remains, and the writer uses the material in its proper context.

10.   Use brackets for secondary asides within parentheses.

Avoid using parentheses and brackets excessively. If you discover the need for an aside within an aside, chances are that the thought is too complex. Consider the alternatives of two or more sentences, a footnote, or a complete division between paragraphs. Always strive for clarity.

When a two-part aside is required, use parentheses as the first level and brackets as the second.

Example:
The agreed-upon amount (defined by the contract as
$20,000 [twenty thousand dollars] and finalized last
month) is now being disputed by the other side.

The example is grammatically correct and follows the style guidelines, but an alternative method of expression can invariably be used to express the same ideas better.

Preferred form:
The agreed-upon amount of $20,000 (twenty thousand

dollars) is now being disputed by the other side. However, the agreement is defined by the contract that was signed last month.

11.   Select parentheses as a first choice.

If the application allows either parentheses or brackets, give preference to parentheses. Use brackets for second-level asides or for other applications to distinguish their use from that of parentheses.

*   *   *

PARTS OF SPEECH

Each segment of a sentence is assigned an identifying label known as a part of speech, each part serving a specific function within the sentence. A study of the parts of speech as they relate to the remainder of the words in a sentence helps form a basic understanding of grammar, expression, and style.

Parts of speech may describe, assert, join, modify, question, and explain.

Adjectives

Adjectives are modifiers. They add to and enhance the significance of nouns and pronouns. When a quality is brought forward with an adjective, it is called a *descriptive* adjective. The alternative is the imposition of boundaries—a *limiting* adjective.

Descriptive adjectives:
an *experienced* manager
the *quarterly* report

The adjective *experienced* describes the noun *manager* in the first example. Without the descriptive adjective, a reader would know only that the discussion involved a manager, without knowing what kind of manager. In the second example, the adjective *quarterly* describes the noun *report*. With the adjective, the reader knows what kind of report is being discussed.

Limiting adjectives:
  a group of *three* managers
  a *partial* report

In these examples, the adjectives limit rather than describe the noun. In the first example, the adjective *three* limits the number of managers under discussion. In the second example, the reader is advised that the report is partial. Neither of these adjectives actually describes the nouns involved.

Descriptive and limiting adjectives can be combined and used together. When this occurs, the limiting adjective almost always appears first. This rule makes sense because the limitation applies not only to the noun but to the descriptive adjective as well.

Limited and descriptive adjectives:
  three experienced managers
  a *partial quarterly* report

1.   Use -*er* and -*est* for comparative and superlative forms.

Adjectives can be expressed in degrees of comparison: positive, comparative, and superlative. One-syllable adjective comparisons are usually achieved by adding the suffix -*er* for comparative form and -*est* for superlative form.

Examples:

Positive	Comparative	Superlative
small	smaller	smallest
big	bigger	biggest
long	longer	longest
short	shorter	shortest

2. Create the comparative and superlative forms of adjectives with more than three syllables by preceding with the words *more* and *most.*

Examples:

Positive	Comparative	Superlative
interesting	more interesting	most interesting
optimistic	more optimistic	most optimistic
profitable	more profitable	most profitable

3. Avoid illogical comparisons.

The rules for comparative expression help avoid redundant forms of expression. Some words cannot be logically compared.

Illogical comparison:
    less unhappy (*happier* or *less sad* would be easier to
        understand and more to the point)

4. Do not use absolute words in comparative form.

Exact and *unique,* for example, are absolute words; they cannot be expressed in comparative form, although examples of such expression occur regularly and frequently in business communications.

Improper comparison:
    This answer is more exact.
    Our product is the most unique of its kind.

Correct comparison:
    This answer is exact.
    Our product is unique.

5. Adjectives are used after verbs denoting the five senses and linking verbs.

A common mistake is to use adverbs when adjectives should be used.

Incorrect form:
> The food smelled strangely.
> The first draft looks roughly.
> That decision appears correctly.
> The western division became profitably this year.

Correct form:
> The food smelled strange.
> The first draft looks rough.
> That decision appears correct.
> The western division became profitable this year.

Adverbs

Adverbs modify verbs, clauses, and other adverbs. Verbs without adjectives can be virtually useless without the use of adverbs. Adverbs identify place, time, manner, and degree of some action.

Adverbs modifying verbs:
> The staff worked *furiously* to meet its deadline.
> The meeting *usually* ended on time.

In the first example, the adverb *furiously* sets the tone for the sentence. Without the adverb, the sentence lacks flavor or degree. In the second example, the adverb *usually* qualifies the verb *ended* by specifying that the meeting does not always end on time, an important distinction in reporting facts.

Adverbs modifying clauses:
> *Undoubtedly,* they will rise to the occasion.
> *Certainly,* we may depend on you.

In both cases, the adverb modifies the action (*rise* in the first case, *depend* in the second case). However, the entire action of the phrase is modified when preceded by an adverb in this manner.

Adverbs modifying other adverbs:
> The improved budget worked *much* better.
> We remained in balance *far* longer.

In the first example, the word *much* modifies the adverb *better*. In the second example, the adverb *far* modifies the adverb *longer*. In many instances, style is clarified by removal of excessive adverbs; however, at times they serve a useful purpose in subtly adding significance and degree to a statement.

Certain adverbs are classified according to the way they qualify a statement (or question). A *conjunctive* adverb joins or qualifies a thought. Typical adverbs in this class are *nevertheless, therefore, however, then, accordingly,* and *consequently.* Another special class are the *interrogative* adverbs: *how, what, where, why,* and *when.*

1. Use adverbs to show degrees of comparison.

Comparison of adverbs follows rules similar to those for comparison of adjectives. One-syllable adverbs are generally compared by adding *-er* in comparative form or *-est* in superlative form.

Examples:

Positive	Comparative	Superlative
slow	slower	slowest
quick	quicker	quickest

Use *more* or *less* (comparative) and *most* and *least* (superlative) to show comparison with adverbs exceeding one syllable. Such adverbs usually end in *-ly.*

Examples:

Positive	Comparative	Superlative
slowly	more slowly	most slowly
	less slowly	least slowly
quickly	more quickly	most quickly
	less quickly	least quickly

Irregular adverbs have their own form of comparison. The best example is the comparative form for *well:* the comparative form is *better* and the superlative form is *best.*

2. Many adjectives can be formed into adverbs simply by adding *-ly* on the end.

Examples:

Adjective	Adverb
significant	significantly
careful	carefully
occasional	occasionally

3. Place adverbs as close as possible to the word being modified.

This rule is especially true for adverbs of degree, such as *only,* *also,* and *almost.*

Incorrect placement:
> The store only sold items marked down.
> Managers also were asked to track absenteeism.
> Our division almost had met its budget.

Correct placement:
> The store sold only items marked down.
> Managers were asked to also track absenteeism.
> Our division had almost met its budget.

Conjunctions

A *conjunction* is a joining or qualifying word. It joins two or more other words, phrases, or clauses in a sentence. The most easily recognized form is *coordinating conjunctions: and, or, but, for,* and *yet.*

Conjunctions joining nouns:
> managers *and* employees
> corporations *and* partnerships

Conjunctions joining phrases:
> the functions of the company *and* of the individual
> to identify *but* not to correct

Conjunctions joining clauses:
> We intend to realize a profit, *but* that will require a
>   change in competitive conditions.
> The meeting will begin on time, *or* we will have to pay
>   more for the hall.

1. Use a *subordinating conjunction* to connect or qualify two different sections of the sentence, which are usually clauses.

This type of conjunction includes words like *before, after, until, unless, although, that,* and *since.*

> *Subordinating conjunctions:*
> Balance the books *after* posting the entries.
> Don't write the letter *unless* the information has arrived.

2. Use *correlative conjunctions* together, although they do not necessarily appear together in the sentence.

Examples of such pairs are *neither-nor, not only-but,* and *either-or.*

> *Correlative conjunctions:*
> *Not only* the division *but* the entire company suffered
>   severe losses.
> *Either* devise systems to capture errors, *or* eliminate them
>   altogether.

Nouns

Nouns are the names of persons, places, and things. Collectively, nouns are classified in two primary groups. *Proper* nouns are specific and are capitalized; *common* nouns are general and are not capitalized unless they appear as the first word of a sentence.

Examples:

Proper	Common
Chicago	city
Robert	man
Mary	woman
Canada	country

Nouns are also described by their attributes:

- *Count nouns:* Describe persons, places, or things that can be specifically counted (e.g., *employees, dollars, typewriters, shelves*).
- *Mass nouns:* The reference is to an inseparable whole (e.g., *money, air, water, sunlight*).
- *Abstract nouns:* Ideas or concepts that are intangible and cannot be counted, seen, or touched (e.g., *patriotism, spirit, dedication, pride, ego*).
- *Concrete nouns:* Can be seen, felt, heard, smelled, or touched (e.g., *dollars, rain, noise, picture*).
- *Collective nouns:* Groups of things in singular form but with a plural identification (e.g., *people, audience, staff, committee*).

1. Avoid style and punctuation errors when distinguishing between a noun's possessive form and its plural form.

As a general rule, a possessive form requires the addition of an apostrophe at the end of the noun, followed by an *s*. The plural form normally requires the addition of an *s* without an apostrophe.

Examples:

Possessive	Plural
manager's	managers
employee's	employees
supervisor's	supervisors

2. Create the possessive for nouns ending in s (including plural form) by adding an apostrophe at the end of the word.

Example:
managers' [possessive for more than one manager]

3. Beware—the language has ample exceptions.

Many nouns in the plural form do not end in s. In those cases, the possessive is formed by adding an apostrophe and an s.

Examples:
women's   men's   children's

4. When referring to multiple persons in one sentence, show the possessive for each.

Examples:
The manager's and employee's responsibilities are invariably connected.
Maria's and Robert's departments are on the same floor.

This rule applies, however, only when the verb implies separation. In the examples above, the structure of the sentences reveals different possessives. The manager's responsibilities are not identical to the employee's responsibilities, and Maria's department is not the same place as Robert's department. Possessives are placed only on the last noun when the verb applies to both nouns.

Verb applying to both nouns:
The manager and employee's responsibilities cannot be logically separated.
Maria and Robert's department is on the second floor.

In both examples, the content of the sentence changed to indicate the sameness of the verbs. In the first example, the verb *responsibilities* is shared by both indicated nouns; and Robert and Mary are in the same department in the second example.

5.   When referring to one individual by title, place the apostrophe and the *s* at the end of the last noun in the title.

Possessives in titles:
The chief financial officer's report was delayed.
The certified public accountant's report approved all of
the books and records as reported.

6.   Form the plural form of most nouns by adding *s*.

Some exceptions should be noted. Nouns ending in *s, z, x, ch,* and *sh* require the addition of *-es* to form a plural.

-es plurals:
We paid more in corporate income *taxes* last year.
The budget *slashes* were devastating.

7.   Form the plural for a noun that ends in the letter *o* and is preceded by a consonant by adding *-es;* however, when a noun ends in *o* and is preceded by a vowel, the plural is formed with an *s* alone.

Examples:
The *echoes* of dissatisfaction were heard.
The *ratios* demonstrated the point quite well.

8.   Irregular nouns do not conform to any rules.

The following list indicates the range of potential plural forms for nouns that cannot be subjected to any clear set of standard rules.

Examples:

Singular	Plural	Singular	Plural
addendum	addenda	axis	axes
basis	bases	crisis	crises
criterion	criteria	datum	data
man	men	matrix	matrices
medium	media	parenthesis	parentheses
radius	radii	symposium	symposia
synopsis	synopses	terminus	termini
woman	women	thesis	theses

9. Form the plural for compound nouns by adding *s* or -*es* is added to the primary descriptive word.

This word may appear as the first, middle, or last word in the compound term.

Examples:
>   assistant financial officers
>   assistants to the president
>   attorneys at law
>   deputy supervisors
>   powers that be

10. Form plurals for acronyms, abbreviations, and some slang expressions by adding *s*.

This exception is widespread in the business environment, where abbreviations and acronyms are in common use.

Examples:
>   ABCs   CEOs   regs

Prepositions

The preposition, a word that links other words or phrases in the sentence, reflects direction, time, or location and is the first word of a prepositional phrase. This phrase consists of the preposition and the object (and, frequently, the object's modifiers).

Prepositional phrases:
> The company is moving *toward* the ultimate goal.
> We prepared the report *for* management.
> Our profits this year are estimated to be *above* the
>   previous year's results.

In the first sentence, the preposition *toward* links the preceding parts of the sentence to the object, *goal*. The adjective *ultimate* also modifies *goal*. The second sentence shows an example of a prepositional phrase with only a preposition, *for,* and an object, *management*. There are no modifiers. The preposition links information about the report to the object following. In the third example, the preposition *above* relates to the object *results*. The words *the previous* and *year's* modify the object *results*.

1.   Use *among* when more than two things are at issue and *between* when only two things are at issue.

A common mistake is the confusion of use for the prepositions *between* and *among*. A simple rule to follow is this: Use *between* when two different things are at issue, and use *among* when more than two things are at issue. In some applications, the more-than-two situation is satisfied by using either word, notably when the precise number is not indicated, but apply the rule consistently to avoid problems.

Examples:
> We had to choose between the two plans.
> Resources are divided among our seven divisions.
> Let's pick the best solution from among all ideas
>   presented. [*Between* could be used, but *among* is
>   preferable.]

2.   Avoid using prepositions if they are not essential to the meaning of the sentence.

As a function of editing, sentences can be made more forceful by the removal of unnecessary words.

Prepositions unnecessary in sentences:
> All *of* the employees attended.
> The departments are too near *to* one another.

3. Do not capitalize prepositions in titles if they contain fewer than four words.

If the preposition is the first word in a title, it is capitalized.

Examples:
> *Of Human Bondage*
> *Applications of Budgeting*
> *Business Without Bosses*

4. Avoid double prepositions and ending sentences with prepositions (often characterized by the following of a preposition with the additional *of*).

Both of these habits weaken style and tend to confuse the meaning of a message.

Misused prepositions:
> We took the numbers *off of* the report.
> The department is *inside of* the building.
> We need to know the report this came *from*.
> They want to know where headquarters is *at*.

Preferred expressions:
> We took the numbers *from* the report.
> The department is *in* the building.
> We need to know *from* which report this came.
> They want to know the location *of* headquarters.

Some exceptions are practical. For example, some sentences ended with prepositions are less awkward than strict adherence to the general rule.

Prepositions at the end of sentences:
The market is worth going into.
This is the report I told you about.
The plan was objected to.

5. Prepositions can be coupled with verbs, adverbs, and adjectives.

Prepositions are sometimes preceded by verbs, adverbs, or adjectives.

Prepositions in nonphrase form:

interested *in*	aware *of*
comply *with*	capable *of*
conform *with* (or *to*)	object *to*

Common simple prepositions:

at	by	in	of
on	of	to	up
for	off	out	down
from	with	through	

Common complex prepositions and phrases:

according to	against
beneath	by means of
in front of	on top of

Pronouns

A pronoun replaces a noun or a noun phrase. This enables expression without the monotony of repeating the noun several times in the course of a paragraph, letter, or essay.

1. Use personal pronouns to replace nouns of people speaking (first person), people spoken to (second person), or persons spoken about (third person).

The three "voices" of personal pronouns are important to ensure proper style. Consistency in the voice used, also known as *point of view,* determines how well focused writing is.

Incorrect voice style:

> I prepared the report from our database, knowing that
> they wanted to see all of the summaries and projections
> we had available. You have to study our report with the
> knowledge of how I proceeded.

Correct voice style in second person:

> We prepared the report from our database, knowing that
> all summaries of available data and projections were of
> interest. The report should be studied with the
> knowledge of how we proceeded.

First person should be reserved for personal letters and memos directed to someone the writer knows. Second person is the most commonly used business style. *We* and *us* may represent a department, a company, or a division. Third person is often mixed with second person when second person alone would be preferable; third person alone tends to become passive.

Second- and third-person references:

> We addressed our correspondence to the correct
> agencies, and their responses were general in nature.
> When we inquired about the original request, they said
> they had never received them.

Preferred form, second person only:

> We addressed our correspondence to the correct
> agencies, whose responses were general in nature.
> When we inquired about the original request, we were
> told it had not been received.

Personal pronouns are further divided into three cases:

> *subjective* case pronoun—the subject of the verb
> *objective* case pronoun—used when the pronoun is the object
> of the verb
> *possessive* case pronoun—used when the form indicates pos-
> session.

The table summarizes personal pronouns in each voice and for each case.

	Subjective	*Objective*	*Possessive*
First-person singular	I	me	my
First-person plural	we	us	our
Second-person singular	you	you	your
Second-person plural	you	you	your
Third-person singular			
Masculine	he	him	his
Feminine	she	her	hers
Neutral	it	it	its
Third-person plural	they	them	their

2. Use demonstrative pronouns to point out or indicate.

There are only four such pronouns and they can be broken down into singular or plural, and distinguished by implied distance: close—*this* (sing.)/*these* (pl.), and far—*that* (sing.)/*those* (pl.).

The close-far distinction is similar to the distinction made in personal pronouns between first and second person. *This* is analogous to *I*, and *that* is analogous to *you*. It is not accurate, however, to assign the characteristic of voice to demonstrative pronouns.

3. Use indefinite pronouns to identify a grouping or classification of people or things.

Examples:

all	either
another	every
any	everybody
anybody	everyone
anyone	everything
anything	few
anywhere	many
both	more
each	most

much	others
neither	several
nobody	some
none	somebody
no one	someone
nothing	something
nowhere	somewhere
one	such

Indefinite pronouns sometimes act as adjectives, depending on their use.

Examples:
   Several employees are absent today.
   Many customers prefer the more expensive model.

Excessive use of indefinite pronouns, especially as adjectives, tends to weaken style. More specific descriptions are invariably preferred.

Less specific descriptions:
   A number of employees are absent today.
   Customers sometimes expressed a preference for the more expensive model.

More specific descriptions:
   Twelve employees are absent today.
   Fifteen percent of customers prefer the more expensive model.

4.   Interrogative pronouns ask a question.

These include words such as *who, whom, what,* and *which.* Some interrogative pronouns are also relative pronouns; they take the place of a noun like other pronouns but also connect a relationship between a main clause and a dependent clause.

Relative pronouns:
   The manager decided *which* report to prepare first.
   We decided *who* to assign the job.

In the first example, the connecting pronoun *which* connects the clauses on either side. In the second example, the pronoun *who* serves the same function. Compared to relative pronouns, an interrogative pronoun, while the same word, serves a different function by merely asking a question without connecting two separate clauses.

Interrogative pronouns:
Which report should be prepared first?
Who should complete this job?

5.   Reflexive pronouns are distinguished by the ending -*self* (singular) or -*selves* (plural).

The list of these pronouns is:

herself	ourselves
himself	themselves
itself	yourself
myself	yourselves
oneself	

One form of reflexive pronoun is the intensive pronoun, which also has the -*self* or -*selves* ending but serves the function of adding emphasis to a statement.

Intensive pronouns:
I *myself* interviewed the candidate.
They *themselves* are accountable.

6.   Reciprocal pronouns involve relationships between items.

Because more than one person or thing must be involved, all reciprocal pronouns are plural. This list includes *each other,* which can mean two only or more than two.

Two only:
> The managers of personnel and accounting work well
> with *each other.*

More than two:
> All of the employees work well with *one another.*

Verbs

The verb describes action in the sentence. An action may be a feeling, a physical movement, a thought, an idea, or even the state of being. (*To be* is one of the most common verbs.)

A *transitive verb* has a direct object. The object and the action of the verb are linked directly.

Transitive verbs:
> The employee *wrote* the report.
> I *see* the street from my window.

In the first example, the report is the object of the verb. In the second example the verb appears earlier in the sentence; still, it has an object, *street.*

In comparison, *intransitive verbs* do not have direct objects. This verb can complete its meaning without needing to relate to another word.

Intransitive verbs:
> The marketing plan *worked.*
> Our employees *reported.*

In the first example, there is no object to finalize the action. The statement is simply made that the marketing plan worked; how, when, or why it worked is not specified. In the second example, there is, again, no object. The employees reported. It does not say when, to whom, or how they reported.

1.   Be aware of verb tenses.

Every verb may be expressed in each tense, as basic, progressive, or passive.

Basic verb tenses:

present: *we speak*
past: *we spoke*
future: *we will speak*
present perfect: *we have spoken*
past perfect: *we had spoken*
future perfect: *we will have spoken*

Progressive verb tenses:

present: *we are speaking*
past: *we were speaking*
future: *we will be speaking*
present perfect: *we have been speaking*
past perfect: *we had been speaking*
future perfect: *we will have been speaking*

Passive verb tenses:

present: *it is spoken*
past: *it was spoken*
future: *it will be spoken*
present perfect: *it has been spoken*
past perfect: *it had been spoken*
future perfect: *it will have been spoken*

The selection of tense helps enliven your writing style and make it rich. Mixing tenses appropriately helps add variety. Consider the variations of tense in the following paragraph:

Variations in tense used correctly:

The problems with profitability in the western division had been brought to management's attention several months ago. We were particularly concerned with the apparent inability of the division to improve cost control procedures or to increase sales volume. We looked at the differences between that division and the more established eastern division, and we located what we thought to be the answer. We now apply to the western division the same control standards in successful practice in the eastern division. We hope that in the next quarter, we will see tangible improvements. We hope to be able to say after this experiment that we had anticipated, planned, controlled, and then implemented the improved conditions.

This paragraph includes a range of tenses, appropriately used. Discussions involve the past, present, and future, as is often the case. Many business applications include this sort of discussion: the problems observed in the past, actions being taken today, and estimates of the effect in the future.

2. Every verb is conjugated.

Conjugation is the expression of a verb in every possible form, allowing for the tense, number, person, and voice. Following is a complete conjugation of the verb *to work:*

Tense	Number	Person	Active Voice	Passive Voice
Present	singular	first	I work	I am worked
		second	you work	you are worked
		third	he works	he is worked
	plural	first	we work	we are worked
		second	you work	you are worked
		third	they work	they are worked
Progressive present	singular	first	I am working	I am being worked
		second	you are working	you are being worked
		third	he is working	he is being worked
	plural	first	we are working	we are being worked
		second	you are working	you are being worked
		third	they are working	they are being worked
Past	singular	first	I worked	I was worked
		second	you worked	you were worked
		third	he worked	he was worked
	plural	first	we worked	we were worked
		second	you worked	you were worked
		third	they worked	they were worked
Progressive past	singular	first	I was working	I was being worked
		second	you were working	you were being worked

		third	he was working	he was being worked
	plural	first	we were working	we were being worked
		second	you were working	you were being worked
		third	they were working	they were being worked
Future	singular	first	I will work	I will be worked
		second	you will work	you will be worked
		third	he will work	he will be worked
	plural	first	we will work	we will be worked
		second	you will work	you will be worked
		third	they will work	they will be worked
Progressive future	singular	first	I will be working	I will have been worked
		second	you will be working	you will have been worked
		third	he will be working	he will have been worked
	plural	first	we will be working	we will have been working
		second	you will be working	you will have been working
		third	they will be working	they will have been working
Present perfect	singular	first	I have worked	I have been worked
		second	you have worked	you have been worked
		third	he has worked	he has been worked
	plural	first	we have worked	we have been worked
		second	you have worked	you have been worked
		third	they have worked	they have been worked

Past perfect	singular	first	I had worked	I had been worked
		second	you had worked	you had been worked
		third	he had worked	he had been worked
	plural	first	we had worked	we had been worked
		second	you had worked	you had been worked
		third	they had worked	they had been worked
Future perfect	singular	first	I will have worked	I will have been worked
		second	you will have worked	you will have been worked
		third	he will have worked	he will have been worked
	plural	first	we will have worked	we will have been worked
		second	you will have worked	you will have been worked
		third	they will have worked	they will have been worked

3. Confusion about singular and plural leads to many problems in the usage of verbs.

The verb should be singular if its subject is singular and plural if its subject is plural. This rule is generally referred to as *agreement*. When subject and verb are separated within the sentence, you can easily fall into the trap of a subject and verb that do not agree.

Incorrect agreement:
The study of impacts for customers were revealing.
The manufacturer of our goods are visiting today.

Correct agreement:
The study of impacts for customers was revealing.
The manufacturer of our goods is visiting today.

4. Look for opportunities to replace weak verbs with strong verbs.

Although weak verbs—for example, *is, are, have, had, was, were, can, has, do,* and *did*—are essential in the language, they tend to lengthen sentences and obscure meaning.

> *Sentence with weak verb:*
>> Our marketing report was presented today.
>
> *Sentence with strong verb:*
>> We presented our marketing report today.

5. Use strong verbs to assert.

Strong verbs may be more difficult to fit into a sentence, but they should be used to assert and provide direct action rather than passive voice.

> *Weak verb statements:*
>> Budgets are put into action by staff.
>> The report preparation is the responsibility of my
>>   department.
>
> *Strong verb statements:*
>> Staff acts on budgets.
>> My department prepares the report.

6. Improve weak verb phrases with stronger replacements.

> *Weak verb phrases:*
>> Employees who work hard . . .
>> Managers who are ambitious . . .
>
> *Strong replacements:*
>> Hardworking employees . . .
>> Ambitious managers . . .

7. Avoid the use of the very specialized subjunctive form of verb in most applications.

You should, however, use the subjunctive form in limited circumstances: when recommending a course of action, when speculating about unknown, uncertain, or untrue conditions, or when presenting a demand.

> *Subjunctive form:*
> Were our estimates correct, we would not be involved
>   today with explaining variances.
> If it were possible, we would increase every employee's
>   pay by that rate.
> We strongly recommend that this matter be settled.
> I insist that we act at once.

See also: ACTIVE AND PASSIVE VOICE; FALSE SUBJECTS

*   *   *

Percentages: *SEE* DECIMALS, FRACTIONS, AND PERCENTAGES

Periods: *SEE* PUNCTUATION

PHOTOGRAPHS

Photographs are used in a broad range of business publications: annual and interim corporate reports, brochures, promotional literature, and reports. They add interest and variety to the text and show readers the topic being discussed. When your report is intended to convince a decision maker, photographs can improve your chances for approval.

If you will be using photographs, you will probably work with a professional photography company or a corporate department. You will have to select from a range of choices.

1.   The subject of the photograph should be framed well.

This does not necessarily mean that the subject must be in the center of the photo; rather, a pleasing balance of light and dark areas is important. Many pictures can be cropped to achieve a more desirable effect.

2.   Photographs must be in focus.

Out-of-focus photos cannot be salvaged and should be rejected.

3.   Avoid overly dark photographs.

When photos are not well balanced in terms of light, they are more distracting than helpful. When choosing from several different photographs, reject those with too many shadows or dark areas.

4.   Be aware that a print can be revised and improved in some situations.

You might find an especially good photograph that is too dark, for example. Consult with the photographer. By varying the exposure time during developing or by exposing different sections of the photo to varying degrees of light (called *ducking*), dark areas can be minimized or eliminated.

5.   Some photos can be flopped: printed in reverse of the true scene.

This should be applied only to nonlandmark scenes, and never to photos with lettering, company buildings, or work sites. Flopping is appropriate when better page balance is achieved with it, and when producing the picture in reverse does not distort or misrepresent what is being reported.

Photo P-1

In many cases a photo is more attractive to the eye if the subject is not precisely centered, as long as there is an effective distribution of light and shadow. This example is lively and well balanced. The diagonal shadows add interest, and the movement of the two people is especially appealing because they are walking toward the camera.

Photo P-2

This is an example of a poor photograph. The camera is too far away to clearly see the faces of the subjects or what they are doing. The large black door in the center and the white vertical line separating two panes of glass (near right edge) present serious compositional problems. Yet cropping them out would leave only a very narrow, claustrophobic image with a dark line straight up the center. For a better photo of this subject, the photographer should have been inside the room with the people.

6.   Be cautious when selecting photographs from color separations, slides, or negatives.

You don't always see accurately what a photograph will look like when viewing only a small, isolated version of it. View photographs through a viewer or projector, and avoid making selections from negatives.

Photos P-1 and P-2 illustrate good and poor photographs, respectively, and explain the various components of them.

*   *   *

PLANNING DOCUMENTS

Organizations develop brief planning statements to serve as guidelines on several levels. First, a company objective statement serves as an overall guide to the organization's purpose. Second, a short-term statement of goals (usually one year or less) sets a course for the immediate future. And third, the same statement of immediate goals serves as a guideline for the development of forecasts and budgets.

1. Keep objective statements brief and direct.

The objective is a brief statement designed to identify the company's purpose. A good way to develop this statement is by identifying the sectors or elements of the organization, typically (1) management, (2) internal staff, (3) vendors or suppliers, and (4) customers.

The objective statement is more easily written once these groups are defined and understood. For example, an organization might identify a list of important objective elements.

Example of important objective elements:
- Recruit the most capable management team
- Hire and train a spirited internal staff
- Find and work with the best vendors
- Work to earn customer loyalty

These basic and simplified examples lend themselves to the development of an objective statement.

Objective statement:
The Sample Corporation applies the skills of its management team with the purpose of hiring and training a professional internal staff. The corporation recognizes the importance of attracting and supporting

a broad range of vendors and suppliers. Finally, the corporation strives to retain and expand its base of loyal, satisfied customers.

2.   Use goal setting for marketing expansion and for departmental programs.

Goals should contain a clear definition, a deadline, and a means for measuring the success of the goal. Goal setting is particularly effective in establishing goals for employees within a department. Establishing a goal, a deadline, and a measure of success enables the employee to operate with a clear definition of the manager's expectations. It also provides the means for performance review.

a.   Definition:

A goal is defined with a brief statement, clearly spelling out what you want to achieve.

Examples:
Revise the filing system completely to conform to the company-wide filing procedure.
Develop a market tracking system that can be automated and put into effect in every branch office.
Reduce expenses by 15 percent or more without loss in efficiency.

b.   Deadline:

Every goal requires a deadline for completion. The deadline should be realistic, with enough time allowed to achieve the goal but within the near future—generally within one year or less—so that everyone involved has some sense of urgency.

c.   Means for measurement:

Goals should be defined in terms of how their success is measured, in order to know whether the goal is successful.

Examples:

> The filing system will be completely in conformity with the
> company-wide system.
> The market tracking system will be in each office, working
> as designed, and personnel in each office will have
> been trained in its use.
> Expenses will be 15 percent or more below current level,
> and work flow will continue at current levels without
> growth in errors.

3. Base forecasts and budgets on specific goals that can be measured.

Goals are useful in the development of budgets and forecasts
and can be used to establish the standard by which a forecast
and budget are to be prepared. Goals should always be written
down.

In forecasting and budgeting, the outcome is measured in
dollars and cents—the easiest method for judging success or
failure of a goal. However, the expected success of a forecasting
or budgetary goal may also be given a range.

> *Goal with a range of outcome:*
> The outcome is either favorable (meaning actual expenses
> are lower than budget) or the unfavorable variance is
> lower than $500 or 5 percent of the budget amount.

Forecasts and budgets, like other forms of goals, are useful
only if the outcome is measured as the period of time continues.
A variation of the six-month or yearly forecast and budget is the
longer-term budget document.

Remember these important points about forecasting:

- The longer the period is that is being estimated, the less
  accurate it will be.
- Without a clearly defined purpose, the work that goes into
  a long-range planning document is of no practical use. The
  purpose should be to make current decisions based on the
  best guess of long-range direction.
- If an organization employs long-range planning tech-

niques, the effort should be updated at least once per year. Even if the only benefit is to observe how long-range perceptions change with time, the effort may have a worthwhile purpose

See also: SAMPLE FORMS SECTION

* * *

POSSESSIVES

A possessive denotes ownership, either literal or more figurative, on the part of the noun.

1. Form the possessive of most singular nouns, proper and common, by adding an apostrophe and the letter *s*.

Examples:
the employee's desk
Sample Company's assets
Hector's attitude
the company's goodwill

2. If a singular noun ends in *s* or *x*, form the possessive by adding an apostrophe and the letter *s*.

Examples:
the boss's absence   the fox's tail

Some guides say that nouns ending in *s* or *x* should be made possessive with the apostrophe alone:

Alternative style:

    the boss' memo   the fox' tail

But this style does not match the way the phrase would be pronounced, so adding the *s* is preferable.

3. If a plural noun ends in *s,* add an apostrophe to form the possessive; if a plural noun does not end in *s,* add an apostrophe and *s,* just as with singular nouns.

The distinguishing mark of the possessive form is the apostrophe and the addition of an *s* to the word. This is usually the case for singular-noun possessives and for plural nouns that do not end in the letter *s.*

Examples:
    the men's jobs
    the children's parents
    the employees' paychecks

When using titles or names of companies in possessive form, add the apostrophe and the *s* to the end of the last word.

Examples:
    the chief financial officer's report
    International Business Machines's stock price

4. Learn possessive forms of personal pronouns.

No apostrophe or *s* is required for possessive adjectives and pronouns, because these words are already expressions in possessive form. These words are:

my	mine
his	his
it	its

our   ours
your   yours
her   hers
their   theirs

*   *   *

PROCEDURES MANUALS

When writing and updating procedures manuals, employ a straightforward writing style. The manual documents work processes and should serve as a training guide. For the purpose of this section, the following definitions are used:

Job: A range of tasks performed by one or more people for the purpose of completing an identifiable result (report, summary, etc.).

Task: A step required in the completion of a job, usually performed by one person.

Routine: a simple task, often performed every day or on a recurring basis each week or month.

Department: The area of responsibility for a specific series of related jobs and tasks.

Desk: The location within a department where the job and its tasks are completed. The term *desk* is used in place of an individual name so that a description will not become obsolete when a person is transferred. Some individual employees also operate in more than one capacity, meaning they execute the jobs and tasks of more than one desk.

1. Select the best approach for preparing the manual.

Some organizations assign the task of developing procedures manuals to one department or person. Others assign the task to the personnel department or a specialized training department, or each individual department may be told to develop its own procedures.

The advantage of centralized procedures is that the task will be performed consistently and has a better chance of being revised and updated regularly. The disadvantage is that a distant individual cannot know the job as well as the person who performs it. Centralized procedures often become obsolete because they are not updated as job performance methods change.

The advantage of having each person do his or her own documentation is knowledge: The person doing the job knows how it is done. The disadvantage is inconsistency. Some people perform the job well; others do not. Procedures will be updated only if employees are reminded to do so. Every manager and supervisor knows that most employees exhibit a high level of resistance to the task of writing.

2. Use outline form.

Use outline form to document the sections of the procedures manual. Design the format of outlining so that all sections can be expanded without limitation. This might mean having to expand the outline references beyond two or three sublevels. As a general rule, outlines are clearer when the number of sublevels is limited; that is not always possible.

Procedures manuals should be organized so that the first outline level indicates the department, the second identifies the section or type of work, and subsequent levels are used for distinguishing specific desks, jobs, and detailed tasks.

3. Employ flowcharts as aids for narrative sections.

Relatively simple tasks, or *routines*, probably need little explanation. A routine performed daily can usually be described in a single paragraph. For example, a routine such as "opening the mail" or "telephoning the supervisor" does not need a visual aid. Routines often occur as part of a more complex task.

For tasks with numerous steps, flowcharts can be useful

explanatory and training tools. (Refer to the Flowcharts section to examine different formatting choices.) Even when using visual aids for a solitary task, take care to indicate (1) points in the task when information or documents must come to the person performing the task, (2) when information or documents must be sent to someone else, (3) the exact point at which documents are to be generated, and (4) all absolute deadlines for completion of the task.

4. Document report generation and deadlines.

Many tasks recur as part of the normal job and do not produce any tangible result; others are designed specifically to complete a form, prepare a report, or post a record. When any form of reporting or documentation is required, the procedures manual should include a line-by-line explanation of (1) the title of the document, (2) a blank sample, (3) a filled-in sample, (4) line-by-line instructions, (5) the desk responsible for completing the document, (6) the deadline and frequency of preparation, and (7) the distribution list.

5. Update references and guidelines.

Each page of the procedures manual and every document sample should include a date at the bottom. This is the origin date for the procedure, form, or document or the latest date that it was revised. It advises anyone reading the procedures manual how recent (or out of date) the section is and may also indicate that there has been a replacement since that date. For example, an employee may know that the procedure for preparing a certain form was changed as of March 1996. All procedures pages in the manual indicate this. The blank form, however, shows a latest revised date of August 1993, and the line-by-line explanations don't make sense either. The employee will know from this information that the sample document is not the right one for the task.

6.   Identify the elements of each task.

A *task* is a series of steps required to complete a segment of a job. Each task, whether shown on a flowchart or explained in a narrative, is defined by a series of actions with a clear starting and stopping point. The reason for identifying every task in a job is to describe what has to be done and advise the employee of the order in which tasks must be completed.

Some tasks, however, can be performed out of order. When working against a deadline, for example, it may be that a certain task has to be held up; however, subsequent tasks may be performed so that time can be saved later. A properly constructed procedures manual will specify when out-of-sequence work can be performed.

Task breakdowns also help trainees to digest information. An especially daunting task is more easily mastered when broken down into understandable, distinct tasks that can be memorized, comprehended, and executed without much difficulty.

7.   Identify the elements of each job.

A job is a series of tasks with a clear beginning and end. The procedures manual should also explain the reason a job is performed. A job description should include an identification of the responsible desk, any deadlines, frequency of performance, documents to be produced as part of the job completion, distribution list, and all needed approvals.

8.   Label all parts of the manual clearly.

All segments of the procedures manual should be marked clearly and separated by index tabs or other devices. Each heading and subheading within the manual should also be readily distinguishable. Anyone opening the manual to a page should be able to identify (1) the department or division, (2) the title of the job and task, and (3) the placement within the overall outline.

9.   Strive for uniformity.

Every department contributing to the procedures manual is expected to comply with the established format, not only for labeling and identification but also for the approach taken in providing documentation. The only way to ensure absolute consistency is to assign one individual to write procedures or rewrite them so they conform in format and style. The most effective procedures are those that conform with other departmental procedures, and can easily be revised and updated. Ultimately, the success of a procedures manual is found when it can be used effectively as a training tool for new or transferred employees.

See also: FLOWCHARTS; SAMPLE FORMS SECTION

*   *   *

Prepositions: *SEE* **PARTS OF SPEECH**

Pronouns: *SEE* **PARTS OF SPEECH**

Proofreading: *SEE* **EDITING AND PROOFREADING**

PROPOSALS

A proposal is similar to some other types of reports in that it presents information. Its distinguishing attribute, however, is that it offers a course of action that management might not have otherwise considered. When a consulting firm presents a proposal, it hopes to convince the company to hire it to perform a job or series of jobs. When a department or individual within the company presents a proposal, he seeks to make a case for a course of action or executive decision.

1.   Format the proposal for convenience.

A proposal should be easy to read. Even someone who does not intend to read the entire document should be able to tell very quickly (1) the topic of the proposal, (2) the importance of or need for what is being offered, (3) the essence of the proposal, which can usually be expressed in one or two sentences, and (4) the request itself.

All of this information may be summarized on the first full page, following a title page. This format enable a reader to discern quickly who sent the proposal and what that person or department wants.

2. Arrange the content for ease of use.

Preface the proposal with the following pages:

1. *Cover page:* Include a title, identification of the person or department responsible for preparing the document, and the date.
2. Table of contents: Include if the proposal is longer than 6 to 10 pages.
3. *First full page:* Summarize the essential elements of the proposal.

Arrange information in the body of the proposal to make the best case. The following sections should be included:

- *Explanation and background:* Explains why this is a good idea and what the important features are that someone should know in order to make the decision.
- *Financial impacts:* A proposal that can demonstrate a savings or recapture of investment has a better chance for approval. This section should not be exaggerated, however. Base pro forma estimates on conservative information.
- *Examples of application,* especially if the proposal seeks changes in procedures, marketing, or utilization of equipment.
- *Supporting information:* Statistical summaries, financial reports, productivity or work analyses, and any other useful information. These data should be included as attachments to the body of the report.

Be sure to cross-reference all sections of the report to important data. If statistical or financial summaries are included in appendixes, label them and refer in the body of the document to the labeled material. Within the proposal itself, also label all graphs, photographs, tables, charts, and other visual aids. Be sure to cross-reference between visuals and the narrative text for maximum effect. Explain the significance of each visual rather than taking up space to tell the reader what he or she can readily observe independently.

3.   Document all facts.

All facts cited in the proposal should be fully documented. If the proposal refers to other publications, include proper citations by way of footnotes. For extensive citations, also include a bibliography at the end of the report.

Use facts sparingly. In the body of the document, make the case for the proposed change or new idea, and put the details in the appendix. Label it and refer text discussions to it for ease of use, but avoid excessive repetition of numerical data within the body of the report.

If statistics are used, include a section documenting the statistical base. This section should contain an explanation of (1) the source for the statistical information, (2) how that information was applied, (3) any special changes made to the data, such as moving averages or selective use, (4) complete details concerning the assumptions used when statistical data were selected, and (5) the conclusions demonstrated by the statistical information. Numerical information is powerful and compelling in a proposal, especially as it relates to the viability of an idea. A proposal that demonstrates the likelihood for the financial success of the proposed idea will probably be approved unless someone successfully challenges the assumptions included in the proposal.

4.   Use graphics.

Visual aids—charts and graphs, tables, or photographs (when appropriate)—help make a proposal interesting and easier to understand. Visuals also help the writer's style, since less narrative is required to prove the case. Visuals should be appropriate to the discussion and simplify the arguments being presented. Graphics are especially important for all numerical information, because the significance of such data is more easily comprehended visually than in the abstract.

As a general rule, the more numerical data there are, the more the proposal will benefit from visual aids. However, the scaling for related charts and graphs should be the same to the extent possible. Different scaling may be used for dissimilar information and may be beneficial as a means for distinguishing between two dissimilar sets of presented information.

See also: CHARTS AND GRAPHS; CITATIONS; PHOTOGRAPHS

* * *

PUNCTUATION

All writing requires punctuation. Various marks indicate singular or plural, possessives, separate ideas, a series of related ideas, asides, quotations, emphasis, the end of a sentence, questions, and subtle variations of ideas.

Apostrophe

1. Use the apostrophe to indicate possessives.

The general rule for singular nouns is to add an apostrophe and the letter *s* to indicate a possessive.

Examples:

> manager's   employee's   company's

2. Indicate possessives for plural nouns ending in *s* by adding an apostrophe to the end of the word.

Examples:

> managers'   employees'

Personal pronouns (*my, your, his, its, our, their*) and personal adjectives (*mine, yours, hers, ours, theirs*) do not require an apostrophe; they are already in possessive form.

3. Use apostrophes in contractions to indicate the omitted letter.

Contractions are informal forms of expression. They should not be used in business letters or reports.

Examples:

Full Form	Contraction
I am	I'm
you are	you're
he is	he's
they are	they're
they will	they'll

4. The apostrophe is used in descriptive terms, such as to denote time.

Example:

> a month's time   a day's work

5. Use apostrophes when numbers, symbols, and abbreviations are included in text.

Common use is moving away from this practice. As a general guideline, use the apostrophe when it clarifies a point; omit the apostrophe when it is not necessary.

Examples:

The #'s indicate numerical value.
When complete, write x's at the bottom.
The 35's are on the assembly line now.

Colon

The colon is used to change the rhythm and thought of the sentence and to signal a change to the reader.

1. Set up displayed lists within narratives with colons.

Example:

The three steps in this process are:
1. Speak directly with the customer.
2. Promise action by a specified date.
3. Follow up and ensure response.

Colons are not generally used in strict outline form. Indentation of subheadings replaces punctuation when not part of a narrative.

2. Colons link connected ideas or expressions with emphasis on the last idea.

Example:

The importance of service cannot be stressed too greatly:
The customer has to come first.

In this example, the colon effectively draws attention to the material following, an affirming statement that follows the first part of the sentence. (A semicolon, in comparison, tends to give equal weight to both sides, and dashes set aside a thought within the sentence.)

3. Use colons for emphasis.

The preceding example, involving a colon to emphasize the second part of a sentence, is typical. Emphasis is even stronger when the same idea is isolated to one word or phrase at the end of a sentence.

> *Example:*
>> We emphasize the need to provide for the single most
>> important part of the marketing equation: the customer.

4. Use a colon at the end of the salutation in business letters.

In informal correspondence and personal notes, the colon is sometimes replaced with a comma or a dash.

> *Formal salutation:*
>> Dear Mr. Anderson:
>
> *Informal salutations:*
>> Dear Andy,
>> Andy—

5. Use colons in a variety of other ways: as separation between hours and minutes in time notation, to separate volumes and pages when referring to publications, to distinguish between primary titles and subtitles, and to separate the two sides of mathematical ratios.

> *Colon used in time notation:*
>> 12:45
>
> *Colon used in volume and page notation:*
>> see *Business Journal* 11:35

Colon used between primary and subtitle:
   Management Science: A Critical Analysis

Colon used to express ratios:
   The current ratio should be 2:1 or better.

Comma

The comma has the greatest number of different purposes among types of punctuation. It can add emphasis, separate several ideas in one sentence, provide clarity, and avoid misunderstanding of the meaning of the sentence.

1. Use the comma to clarify meaning.

When a sentence or phrase can be interpreted in more than one way, use a comma to help the reader understand.

Unclear meaning:
   The budget committee disagreed with increases and
      proposed revisions.

Clarified meaning:
   The budget committee disagreed with increases, and
      proposed revisions.

In the first example, it is not clear whether the committee's disagreement included proposed revisions. With the inserted comma, the two thoughts are made clear: The committee disagreed with increases, and it proposed revisions.

2. Commas signal the separation of two complex thoughts separated by a conjunction.

Two relatively simple ideas do not require commas.

Complex thoughts with conjunctions:
   The accounting review included discussions of numerous

footnotes about contingent liabilities, and procedures in
inventory valuation that increased net profits.

Simple thoughts not requiring a comma:
The review included discussions of contingent liabilities
and inventory valuation.

The comma is also used when a sentence contains three or
more ideas. Use a comma following the conjunction to avoid
confusion.

Example:
The process includes initial review, preparation of the
report, and approval.

Do not attempt to join two clauses with a comma only. The
conjunction or semicolon is required.

Two clauses without a conjunction:
Employees generally locate information, prepare the
report.

Corrected sentence with conjunction:
Employees generally locate information and prepare the
report.

3.   Use commas for direct addresses within sentences and for short words or phrases that break the primary idea or expression.

Examples:
The report, Mary, is due tomorrow.
The budget, incidentally, was never completed.

4.   Separate a parenthetical expression within a sentence by commas.

Such expressions are often handled with dashes or parentheses;
however, the comma will suffice without breaking up the flow
of the sentence.

Example:
> Mr. Mackay, according to the biographical data, is an
> experienced executive.

5. Identify introductory elements at the beginning of sentences, whether single words or entire phrases, with commas.

Exceptionally long prepositional phrases serve as qualifying or introductory statements and should also be followed by a comma. Introductory interjections should also be followed by commas.

Examples:
> Incidentally, the meeting has been postponed.
> In spite of all our efforts, we did not succeed.
> Yes, the budget is complete.

6. Use commas to divide numbers above 999 into groups of three.

Whole numbers should be lined up on the far right; dollars and cents or decimals should be lined up on the decimal point.

Examples:
> 1,000
> 999
> 33.56
> 1,223,500.03
> 216,480

7. Separate adjectives by commas when there are more than two; however, do not separate the final adjective from a noun that follows.

Examples:
> It was a brief, informative meeting.

We want to develop a program providing for sincere, responsive, and memorable service.

8. Use commas to indicate omitted words in sentences.

Example:

Most divisions showed a profit; two, a loss.

9. Place a comma in a city and state address following the city name.

Examples:

Duluth, MN
San Francisco, California

10. Place commas in dates following the number of the day.

Use a comma after the year.

Examples:

May 14, 1997
On January 3, 1996, the revised procedures manual was distributed.

11. When material in a sentence is placed within parentheses or brackets and a comma follows the thought preceding, the comma belongs outside the parentheses.

Incorrect placement:

The vice president (Ms. Green,) an expert on the topic, explained.

Correct placement:
> The vice president (Ms. Green), an expert on the topic, explained.

12. When stating a person's last name first, followed by first name, place a comma in between.

Typical applications include file identification.

Examples:
> Andrews, Mark
> Combs, Dr. Andrea
> Smith, Mark Jr.

13. Place a comma between a person's name and title when the name comes first.

Examples:
> Dr. Combs, vice president of research, explained why the marketing idea would not work.
> Mark Smith, manager of the accounting section, delivered the briefing at the finance meeting.

14. Use commas correctly with quotations.

When a quotation is part of a sentence, use a comma after the introductory text.

Example:
> The speaker said, "No one can predict accurately what will occur more than two months out, even with the best data."

Do not use commas for indirect quotations.

Example:
> The speaker said that no one could predict beyond two months with any degree of accuracy, even with the best data.

When the quotation ends with a comma, place the comma before the closing quotation mark.

Example:
> The speaker said, "No one can predict accurately what will occur more than two months out," and that the quality of data will not affect that problem.

Dash

The dash is often used for emphasis within a sentence—either to set apart a thought or to enclose a thought or aside within the middle.

1. Indicate emphasis with repetition using dashes.

Example:
> We were pleased to note an increase in this quarter's profits—a significant increase.

2. Use dashes with end-of-sentence matter to complete a thought or contradict a presumed conclusion.

Examples:
> It is fairly easy to budget expenses for a full year—according to the theory.
> Some managers like to forecast five years ahead—although meaningful long-term forecasting is virtually impossible.

3. Set up parenthetical material within the sentence with a dash, which acts much as a comma does.

Dashes provide much greater emphasis than commas because they break up the thought and the appearance of the sentence.

Parentheses can also be used in this situation, but that technique provides the least amount of emphasis.

Commas used for parenthetical material:
The reason for marketing strategy, profits, cannot be ignored in our planning.

Dashes used for greater emphasis:
The reason for marketing strategy—profits—cannot be ignored in our planning.

4. Follow a quotation with a dash to identify the author.

Example:
"The lion and the calf shall lie down together, but the calf won't get much sleep."—Woody Allen

Ellipses

Ellipses consist of a series of three periods (ellipsis points), each separated by a space, used to indicate an omission of material.

1. Use ellipses in quoted material to signal that some material has been excluded.

Ellipses tell the reader that a direct quotation is not complete.

Original paragraph without exclusions:
The most significant finding by Dr. Harold and his crew of volunteer interns, none of whom wavered in their loyalty even once, was that employees develop opinions independent of the company's published, official statements.

Quotation with ellipses:
"The most significant finding . . . was that employees

develop opinions independent of the company's . . .
official statements.''

2.   When a quotation begins and ends in the middle of a sentence, do not use ellipses at the beginning or end of the quotation.

Original sentence:
Susan realized the flaw in her thinking after she reviewed
the data.

Quotation:
Susan told me she ''realized the flaw'' finally.

3.   In mathematical notation, ellipses express an unknown or unspecified longer list.

Example:

$$(x1 + x2 + . . . xn)$$

Exclamation Mark

The exclamation mark expresses surprise, irony, or strong feelings. In certain advertising, it is used for emphasis.

Examples:
Sale! Three days only!
Hah! I doubt that very much.
Impossible!

1.   Use the exclamation mark rarely in business correspondence.

2.   Place punctuation correctly.

When used within a quotation, the quotation marks should follow the exclamation mark. When used with a question mark, the exclamation mark is placed first.

Examples:
"Reform Now!" was the title of the article.
What!?

Hyphen

The hyphen serves as a connector in certain words or to show a range.

1. Use hyphens as connectors for some words.

Hyphens used as noun connectors:
follow-up
commander-in-chief
ex-employee

Hyphens used as adjective connectors:
year-round controls
month-to-date expense
error-prone shift

Hyphens used as verb connectors:
I will single-space the letter.
Be sure to spot-check the warehouse.
Let's double-time this task.

2. Use hyphens to separate words that are joined to form a new word.

This is common in technical writing, although some everyday usage and business style will also employ the technique.

Hyphens used to create new words:
accounting-style worksheets
marketing-intensive activities
employee-oriented programs

3.   Hyphens indicate a range.

Examples:
   0-100 [zero to one hundred]
   5-10 minutes [five to ten minutes]
   8%-10% [eight to ten percent]
   4-6 employees [four to six employees]

4.   Hyphens appear in numbers between 21 and 99 when those numbers are spelled out.

Examples:
   twenty-seven   four hundred thirty-six

5.   Use hyphens in two- or three-word modifiers expressing the same thought and preceding nouns.

As a general rule, if either modifier could work without the other, hyphens are not used. A hyphen is not used when the same modifiers follow the noun. No hyphen is used for adjective modifiers ending in *-ly*.

Examples:
   A year-to-date report was prepared.
   Do you have figures on our profits, year to date?
   A well-informed director is what this division needs.
   Dr. Cooke is well informed.
   We received a new metal desk.
   We received a newly purchased desk.

6.   Hyphens are used for certain noun prefixes, such as *cross-, ex-, half-, quasi-,* and *self-.*

Many other common prefixes that should be closed up are often hyphenated incorrectly, such as *anti-, mid-, pre-, sub-,* and *un-.*

Exception: To avoid a double vowel, sometimes even these pre-fixes are hyphenated. Consult a dictionary for specific cases.

Hyphenated noun prefixes:
Be sure to *cross*-reference your report thoroughly.
Most job applicants feel *self*-conscious.
An *ex*-employee telephoned for a reference.
He has always been *anti*-intellectual. [to avoid double vowel]

Closed-up noun prefixes:
The entries arrived *post*closing.
The *pre*budget expense was posted last year.
The survey revealed that many people in this company feel *under*employed.
That group is *anti*marketing.

7. Hyphens indicate word breaks at the end of lines.

When text breaks at the end of the line occur in the middle of a word, the hyphen indicates the continuation on the following line. This break must occur at one of two places: (1) the end of a syllable or (2) the hyphenated point in a word. Use a dictionary to check syllabification.

Examples:
We met for lunch at twelve-thirty that day.
The timing of the report coin-cided with the meeting.

Period

Periods serve numerous functions, especially in business communications. When narrative and numerical expressions are mixed, periods can appear in several forms within one paragraph.

1.   The period, also called a "full stop," is used at the end of all sentences that are not questions or exclamatory statements.

2.   When a quotation ends with a period, the quotation mark follows the period.

When unquoted material follows in the same sentence, the period is changed to a comma.

Examples:
> The speaker said, "All in good time."
> "All in good time," the speaker said.

3.   As a general rule, periods are placed outside parentheses and brackets.

The exception is when a full sentence is placed within the enclosed area.

Examples:
> We prepared an annual report (last year).
> The report was prepared on an annual basis. (It was
>   finalized a month ago.)

4.   Periods follow titles and initials; they sometimes but not always follow abbreviations, and they do not follow acronyms.

Examples:
> Acct. dept. mngr.
> Mr. Anderson
> Dr. Smith
> T. R. Jones
> mktg.
> AMA
> AMACOM

5. Periods are used as decimal points for numbers and to indicate a division between dollars and cents.

Examples:
The variation was 4.332 on the scale.
On average, 4.3 employees resign each year.
The total came to $1,336.32 last month.

6. Periods are used as part of numbered or lettered sections and subsections in outline form or in lists.

Examples:
1.
2.
3.

a.
b.
c.

7. Avoid placing periods after incomplete sentences.

Incomplete sentence:
The report, which was prepared yesterday. It was
    delivered to everyone on the list.

Corrected expression:
The report, which was prepared yesterday, was delivered
    to everyone on the list.

8. Periods end sentences that serve as indirect questions.

Examples:
The manager asked whether the budget was above or
    below actual expenses.
We wondered what was meant by the message.

Question Mark

1.   The question mark ends a direct interrogatory sentence.

Examples:
Is this the correct department?
Where should the work be done?

2.   The question mark is used to end a declarative sentence that contains a question.

This is an awkward style, however. A more assertive form should be used to avoid weakening the message.

A question within a sentence:
Each department is responsible, is it not, for completing its
assigned tasks?

Improved style:
Each department is responsible for completing its
assigned tasks. Isn't this the case?

3.   The question mark is used when a question is placed in the middle of a sentence.

This method of expression should be avoided.

A question mark within a sentence:
How should be the product be marketed? is the important
question.

Improved style:
The important question is: How should the product be
marketed?

4.   Indicate that a declarative sentence is meant to serve as a question with a question mark.

Examples:
The books are balanced?
The shift is over?

5.   The question mark follows an exclamation mark when both are used.

Such usage is rare in business.

Example:
> How could Apex get its product to market faster than we did!?

6.   The question mark should remain inside parentheses or quotation marks when part of the expression.

When the enclosed material is an aside to a larger interrogatory sentence, the question mark is placed outside the parentheses.

Question mark with quotations:
> "Why this course?" asked the speaker.

Question mark with parentheses:
> The shift's defects have increased (why has this occurred?) over the past three months.
> Why have the shift's defects increased in the most recent study (three months)?

7.   Use the question mark to indicate that some material is questionable or unclear.

Examples:
> The report claimed a 450 percent increase in productivity(?).
> He reported that 43 out of 50 cases were positive and exceeded expectations(?).

Quotation Marks

1.   Enclose direct quotations within quotation marks.

Example:
> Jerry said, "There is no time like the present."

2. Use quotation marks when citing material only for directly quoted sections.

Use ellipses or brackets to indicate any exceptions to this rule.

> *Complete passage:*
> Only a small number of all customers included in this survey were willing to participate in the study. This small response indicates that the request itself was perceived as too time-consuming or otherwise inconvenient.

> *Direct quotation:*
> The study failed because "only a small number of all customers" agreed to take part. The testing organization speculated that the test was perceived as "too time-consuming or otherwise inconvenient."

> *Ellipses and brackets use within quotations:*
> "Only a small number . . . were willing to participate . . . [indicating that the test would be] too time-consuming or otherwise inconvenient."

3. When a quotation appears within another quotation, use single quotation marks for the secondary quotation.

> *Example:*
> "We took the action based on the words of our mentor, who warned, 'Inaction is the worst action.' This guided us in all of our decisions and kept us moving forward."

4. Titles of articles in periodicals, chapters of books, songs, poems, and other short published material are enclosed in quotation marks.

> *Example:*
> Did you read this article, "Why I Love My Job So Much," in today's paper?

Titles of longer works (books, magazines) are italicized.

5. Draw attention to words or phrases that are odd or used in exceptional ways with quotation marks.

Example:
> The applicant responded that he was "buzzed" by the possibility of being selected for the position.

Be sure not to overdo this style, however.

6. Place punctuation correctly.

Periods and commas belong inside quotation marks and colons and semicolons outside quotation marks. Question marks and exclamation marks should go inside quotation marks if they are part of the quotation itself; otherwise, they go outside.

Examples:
> He said, "Send the report directly to me."
> "Sure, I'd be glad to," I answered.
> I don't know what they meant by "model employees"; Georgia and Kate were far from that in my opinion.
> I wanted to meet "the big boss": the one Sally had told me so much about.
> "Were they able to repair the computer system in time?" she asked uneasily. [Question mark goes inside quotation marks because it is part of the quoted sentence.]
> What do you think he really meant by "corporate reorganization"? [Question mark is not part of quoted material, so it goes after quotation marks.]
> "You'll never guess who I just saw!" exclaimed Julie.
> But I was harried and wished she would stop distracting me with her "fascinating day"!

7. Quotation marks are sometimes used to indicate "same as material directly above."

This is to be confined only to strictly informal applications, such as worksheets, and never to be incorporated in reports or letters.

Examples:
Account 1234 is in balance.
"   1236 " "   "
"   1239 " "   "

Semicolon

The semicolon is an alternative to the period in some cases. It connects two thoughts that could serve as independent sentences but are related enough that a semicolon is justified.

1.   Semicolons may connect thoughts that, while related, need to be qualified by connecting words.

This is usually the case when the second part of the thought is contradictory.

Example:
Shift defects increased by 13 percent during the month, which alarmed management; however, the managers were not aware of the high volume of trainees during the period.

2.   Use semicolons in a narrative listing when some of the items in the list include commas.

When several items are listed but some segments of the lists include commas, the semicolon clarifies the meaning.

Example:
The marketing department has recommended that budgets include allowances for training seminars; orientation meetings for continuing education, product updates, and practice management; and production of a higher volume of sales literature.

Slash

The slash, also called a *solidus, virgule, slant line, bar,* or *shilling sign,* is used in a wide variety of applications. Be cautious in its use. When it is used carelessly, its intended meaning can be lost.

1. Use a slash to replace the word *per.*

Examples:
price/share [price per share]
cost/employee [cost per employee]

2. Use the slash in abbreviated forms of dates.

This is an informal style for personal notes and interoffice memos; it is also used on worksheets involving dates and values.

Examples:
3/16/97
4/10

3. Used the slash in mathematical expressions to signify division.

In business applications, this style may apply in equations as well as in ratios; both examples involve dividing the first number by the second.

Examples:
$B/12 \times r = M$
2/1 ratio

4. Denote the division between lines of poetry with slashes.

Example:
Our recommendation not to proceed with this marketing

plan is based on the belief that it will not be a profitable venture. As Shakespeare put it, "We go to gain a little patch of ground / That hath in it no profit but the name."

See also: PARENTHESES AND BRACKETS

*   *   *

Question Mark: *SEE* PUNCTUATION

QUOTATIONS

Quotations are another author's words, used judiciously in reports and other documents to bolster your own work.

1.   Place material in quotation marks when quoting exactly.

An indirect quotation should not be represented as anything else.

Direct quotations:
> The government report called attention to "exceptional levels of productivity" last quarter.
> The report was extremely negative, highlighting the "blatant disregard for the comfort of the customer."

Indirect quotations:
> The government report emphasized that production levels were exceptional last quarter.
> The extremely negative report highlighted what it considered a blatant disregard for customer comfort.

2.   Strive to use quotations only in context.

Facts can be misrepresented if they are presented out of context.

Misrepresented facts:
> The government report admitted that production levels
> were "exceptional," which is no guarantee that such
> outcomes should be expected in the future.

In this example, a positive report is used to represent inaccurately that the information was negative concerning the future.

> Lower-than-expected production volume was blamed on
> "complete breakdown of machinery" during the shift.
> However, results in comparison with other shifts cannot
> be disputed.

This type of reporting should be avoided in business applications. Obviously, the complete breakdown of machinery is extraordinary and should not be overlooked in the interest of a purely numerical conclusion. In this situation, the phrase placed in quotation marks shows how the technique can be misused. The tone of the paragraph implies that the quoted material is inaccurate or distorted; in reality, the conclusion of the writer distorts the real problem.

3. Cite the source of the quotation.

Merely placing words within quotation marks is not enough. The source must be given as well.

Missing citation:
> An examination of the "productive business base" is the
> best means for locating likely future profits.

Proper citation:
> According to Dr. Mather's 1995 study, an examination of
> the "productive business base" is the best means for
> locating likely future profits.

4. Place punctuation marks within the quotations if they are part of the quotation.

Periods, question marks, and other punctuation should be included as long as the original wording included them as well.

5.   Quote only as much as needed.

Use ellipses when omitting part of a larger quotation. Some quotations contain the relevant material needed to make a point but also other information that adds nothing to the point being made. In such cases, exclude unnecessary sections, while taking care to preserve the original meaning.

> *Example text:*
> The proper method for selecting sample data will depend on the purpose and use intended. Statistical bases have to be valid if the outcomes are to be of any value. Take great care that your selection does not create a false conclusion.

> *Improperly edited quotation:*
> The report warns that even "the proper method for selecting sample data will . . . create a false conclusion."

> *Properly edited quotation:*
> The report warns that the selection method "will depend on the purpose and use . . . if outcomes are to be of any value."

6.   When a misspelled word, an error in grammar, or a confusing expression is included in the quoted source, do not correct it.

Follow a confusing section or word with [*sic*] enclosed in brackets, which means "so" or "as it was said."

> *Grammatical error in original source:*
> The report concluded that "the database of employees were [*sic*] considered to be broad enough to validate the study."

> *Confusing statements:*
> The report concluded, "None of the data compiled, analyzed, studied, dependably indicated a definitive nor conclusive outcome which could be used [*sic*]."

"We reported that we were advised of what decisions
had been made in place of the correct procedure,
taking place in the absence of the usual group [*sic*]."

See also: CITATIONS; FOOTNOTES; PUNCTUATION

*   *   *

Quotation Marks: *SEE* PUNCTUATION

REDUNDANCY AND REPETITION

1. Avoid using unnecessary words in business text.

Business writing style (like all other writing) should be to the
point. Even the best writers must guard against bad habits in
their writing, and redundancy is one of the most common.

> *Redundant wording:*
> It is absolutely urgent to reach a final conclusion
> concerning the report enclosed herein. The proposed
> recommendations address the issues about basic
> fundamentals in our procedural methods.

> *Tightened wording:*
> We urgently need to reach a conclusion concerning the
> enclosed report. The recommendations address the
> basics in our procedures.

The second example is clearer and more concise than the first.
The redundant phrases add nothing to the message and, in fact,
detract from it.

2.   Examine all writing as part of your self-editing, seeking words that can be eliminated.

This process helps to avoid the use of redundancies while improving your writing style. Apply these style guidelines.

- Nothing can be *absolutely* essential, *attached* together, or *entirely* destroyed. The highlighted words are unnecessary.
- Many sentences can have two or three words eliminated without any change in meaning.
- Almost every communication can be expressed in a shorter, simpler way.
- The tendency in business to obscure or to use more complex methods of explanation is misguided. Readers appreciate simple, well-written, well-communicated reports, letters, and memos.

3.   Be aware of repetition.

The selective use of repetition can be an effective way to add emphasis to writing, but it often denotes the writer's uncertainly that the essence of the message has been expressed.

Effective repetition:
  Markets are the key. Markets are survival. Markets are the
  business of business.

This example employs two forms of repetition. Used in a speech, for example, the audience hears the speaker and realizes that markets are the message. In addition, the slogan "the business of business" is a useful and effective way of emphasizing the point.

Repetition used ineffectively:
  We would like to see this change in procedure if
  management agrees with our premise. The procedure
  changes we are recommending will reduce costs. We
  really need to make a change in the procedure.
  Otherwise, we will still have budget variances if the
  procedure is not changed.

Rewritten statement:
> This change in procedure is recommended as a method
> for reducing costs and saving money.

In the ineffective repetition example, a reader would believe that the writer lacks confidence that the message is coming through clearly. The resultant style is poor and unconvincing.

See also: EDITING AND PROOFREADING

* * *

REPORTS

A variety of specialized reporting formats is used in business, often depending on the nature of the business or the topic of the report itself. The essential style rule for reports is that the design, length, and detail of each one should be based on its purpose and the audience.

1. Recurring reports always follow the same format.

Such documents as progress or monthly reports always use the same format so that readers know where to find information. The format should be determined specifically by the contents and the requirements of the report.

2. Changing a report's format is not a matter for one individual to make in isolation.

The entire readership of the report should be advised of proposed changes and their reasons, and given the opportunity to disagree or to provide ideas to improve a new format. Chances are that changing a report's format will require approval; be certain that the proposed change in format is done with complete documentation and through proper channels. Following are guidelines for suggesting changes in a report's format:

1. Explain the deficiencies in the current format.
2. Provide a cost analysis for the project. Consider existing supplies of blank forms, if applicable; changes in data-bases utilizing the report in its present format; and af-fected departments and how their needs are better ad-dressed by the improved format.
3. Make a specific recommendation for the newly formatted report, including an example. When practical, present the most recently prepared version of the report in the new format, so that improvements are clear.

3. The proposal is a specialized report.

A proposal discusses a one-time idea and therefore has no set format to follow. However, since the proposal puts an idea in front of a decision maker, some important formatting rules should always be followed in the proposal.

1. *A summary.* The first page should summarize what is being proposed, along with the major benefit for making the suggestion. A decision maker will then be able to judge quickly whether the overall idea appears to have merit.
2. *Problem presentation and the proposed solution.* Avoid merely presenting problems and expecting the decision maker to arrive at the solution. The report preparer's job is to present the answer as well as the question.
3. *The conclusion.* End with a brief summary of the key points made on the first page and answer these questions: What is the initial cost of the proposal? How are various departments affected? How long will the transition take? What are the long-term savings, in terms of both effi-ciency and time?
4. *Supplementary or supporting data.* Include this material in an appendix, clearly cross-referenced to the applicable section of the report.

4. Follow general rules for report organization.

- *Number the pages of the report.* Unless the report is only two or three pages long, numbered pages are essential. For especially long reports, include a table of contents to show the reader at a glance what the report includes and to help him or her find the most important information quickly.

- *Place summary conclusions at the front.* The summary page is the most important part of the report, and it should come first. It gives the reader an immediate, easy-to-find overview of the report's essential contents and recommendations.
- *Minimize the body of the report.* Employ a professional, straightforward writing style to keep the section as short as possible and communicate clearly.
- *Provide details in an appendix.* The actual body of the report should contain as few pages as possible, with narratives devoted to interpretation of details, recommended actions, and critical information the reader needs. When reference is made to financial reports, statistical studies, and other material, include the details in the appendix. Keep the body of the report as clear of such details as possible.
- *Use appropriate graphic aids.* Include a listing of all graphs, tables, and other visuals in the table of contents if there are more than two or three such examples.

5. If the report contains references to other sources, include a bibliography.

The bibliography should follow the correct citation style (see Citations). Bibliographic notes should be indicated by number or, if limited in scope, by way of footnotes on each page. If the report includes several detailed sections, reference notes should be summarized at the end of each section.

6. Provide cross-references to all graphics and all material in the appendix.

If the report contains more than one type of graphic, referencing should be distinct. If the report contains more than one section, the sections should be numbered separately, and graphic references should correspond. For example, the first table in section

3 should be numbered "Table 3-1." The fourth table in section 5 should be numbered "Table 5-4." Narrative references should be included within parentheses and may be capitalized for emphasis.

Examples:
> The actual year-to-date results compared to forecast are shown in FIGURE 2-1.
> A complete detailed listing of budget assumptions and content is included in the appendix (page 47, "Budget Assumptions and Worksheets").

See also: CHARTS AND GRAPHS; CITATIONS; FINANCIAL REPORTS; MANUSCRIPTS

*   *   *

Semicolon: *SEE* PUNCTUATION

SENTENCES

The language consists of a series of sentences, strung together in paragraphs and conveying a string of thought. Each sentence expresses an idea that makes sense in the context of material before and after that sentence. A well-constructed essay, memo, letter, or report follows these guidelines, with its sentences building upon each other so that the ideas are expressed clearly.

1.   A simple sentence expresses one idea or complete thought.

Such sentences contain one subject and one verb only. The simple sentence is easily identified. It cannot be broken down into two or more other sentences without changing its meaning.

Examples:
> The marketing analysis was late.
> The employees are in the lunchroom.
> Our seminar began today.

The designation *simple* means only that a single idea or thought is contained within the sentence. Some simple sentences meet this standard while being complex in the information conveyed. They may contain grammatical variations while remaining simple in construction.

Examples:
> It was not a very long meeting. [the noun is a predicate nominative]
> We provided them with a copy of the report and with some implementation ideas. [contains two direct objects and one indirect object]
> The personnel department is located on the seventh floor, at the end of the hall. [contains two prepositional phrases]
> Managers and supervisors need vacations, too. [contains compound subjects]
> The efficiency expert lost his notebook and broke his stopwatch. [contains a compound predicate]

2. A compound sentence combines more than one thought that, by itself, would constitute a complete sentence.

The thoughts (also called *independent clauses,* because they can stand independently) are connected by a conjunction or a semicolon. Unless the two clauses are very short, a comma should precede the conjunction combining them.

Examples:
> The report about staying on schedule was late, so the meeting ran over its allotted time.
> Our seminar ended today, and we hope to stay in town for some sightseeing.
> I report to George, and he reports to Cynthia.
> The employees are in the lunchroom; they are discussing the recent announcement.

3. A complex sentence contains a primary and a subordinate idea (also called *independent* and *dependent clause*).

The independent clause is a complete sentence that can stand alone; the dependent clause does not meet that standard.

Examples:

The meeting was set up when the report was completed.
(*The meeting was set up* is a full sentence on its own;
when the report was completed is not.)
The employees are in the lunchroom, having ensured that
the telephones are still being covered in their
department.
Our seminar began today, even though a holiday
weekend just began.

4. A minor sentence is an afterthought or addition to the sentence preceding it.

The minor sentence is not actually a complete sentence but a limited number of words added on.

Examples:

Was it important that the marketing analysis was late?
How late?
The supervisor has suggested the radical approach of
hiring outside services, arguing that we will spend less
money than if we hire employees. Unlikely.

There is much debate concerning whether a so-called minor sentence is grammatically allowable, especially in business writing. Some believe that these phrases are allowable in spoken English or in dialogue but inappropriate for business memos and letters. The opposite view is that the one- or two-word phrase, when used selectively, adds great emphasis and does have an appropriate usage, even in business documents. The examples illustrate this point. Unless fragments are used excessively, they can be most powerful writing tools.

In addition to adding emphasis, minor sentences break up narratives and help vary the rhythm of the text. Everyone in business who has been exposed to long reports and analyses welcomes some variety in form. This is true for both analytical reports and reports designed to try to influence an executive to make a decision.

Consider this example: You have an idea that management has resisted for some time, even though you have argued that it will save money. Now you're writing a report meant to convince the president that it's a good idea. You start out your report with one of the following paragraphs:

Alternative first paragraphs:

This report proposes a complete change in departmental procedures. While expensive to implement at first, we intend to show that the idea will ultimately save money, not just for the short term, but permanently.

Saving money is a primary purpose of our budgetary and review procedures. Here's an idea that we believe achieves that objective. For an initial investment that is reasonable in perspective, we will be able to reduce costs permanently.

Money. That's what the company will save by implementing this idea. This report proves that the investment we are suggesting will be recaptured within twelve months and create permanent savings from that point forward.

The third paragraph might be considered a hard sell, and placing the one-word sentence at the front is certainly a gimmick—but perhaps an effective one. Be open to the possibility of using the minor sentence for emphasis or effect.

5. Declarative sentences are statements of opinion or fact.

Examples:
The marketing analysis is late.

The employees are in the lunchroom.
Our seminar began today.

6. Interrogative sentences ask questions.

They usually begin with words such as *who, what, when, why, where, how,* and *have.*

Examples:
Why is the marketing analysis late?
Where are the employees?
When does our seminar begin?

7. Exclamatory sentences express surprise and end with an exclamation mark.

Such sentences are rarely used in business communications.

Examples:
Where is the marketing analysis? Late again!
To the lunchroom!
Let's go! The seminar is starting.

8. Imperative sentences are commands, even if politely phrased ones.

They usually begin with a verb.

Examples:
Get me that marketing analysis, please.
Go to the lunchroom as soon as possible.
Start the seminar on time.

9. Vary sentence rhythm so that the reader does not lose interest.

Reading a series of sentences of the same approximate length is boring; the reader may struggle to maintain a string of thought or to comprehend the intended message.

Sentences with identical rhythm

> The marketing analysis is late again. This happens just about every month. I checked the marketing department to ask why. The employees weren't there just now. They are all in the lunchroom. We need an answer as soon as possible. The information is supposed to be presented at the seminar. It is starting today.

Sentences with varied rhythm:

> The marketing analysis is late again, as it seems to be every month. I checked the marketing department. All of the employees are in the lunchroom right now. We need an answer as soon as possible, for presentation at today's seminar.

10. The run-on sentence does not stop at the end of one thought.

It is difficult to read a run-on sentence because it strings several thoughts together without pause. Consequently the reader is unable to divide the thoughts into logical segments or to comprehend the message easily.

A run-on sentence:

> The marketing analysis is late again, which happens just about every month and I checked the marketing department to ask why but the employees weren't there just now because they are all in the lunchroom and we need an answer as soon as possible as the information is supposed to be presented at the seminar, which is starting today.

Another type of run-on sentence is simply wrong in the grammatical sense, consisting of two or more thoughts connected without proper punctuation or attachment by way of conjunctions.

Example:

> The store opened at the usual time there were no customers there that early we didn't expect any.

11.   Avoid sentence fragments by recogniz-ing phrases and clauses.

Phrases and clauses are not complete sentences, though they may contain the wording of complete sentences. In order for a sentence to be complete, the subject has to be accompanied by its own verb, and the thought has to be complete.

> *Sentence fragments:*
> Looking at the budget with a fresh point of view.
> Heading for the seminar with the intention of learning many new management skills.
> Our president, who hails from Minnesota.
> The meeting scheduled for the third Thursday of each month.

> *Revisions to make complete sentences:*
> We are looking at the budget with a fresh point of view.
> Heading for the seminar, I intend to learn many new management skills.
> Our president hails from Minnesota.
> The meeting is scheduled for the third Thursday of each month.

By studying each example set, you can see the flaws and missing components of the clauses and phrases. In the first example, there is no subject for the verb *looking.* The same is true of the second example. In the third, the subject, *president,* has no verb; the problem is corrected by removing a word. The last example is yet another instance of the more common problem of subjects without related verbs. Adding the verb *is* fixes the problem.

12.   Signal the beginning and end of sen-tences correctly.

The first word of every sentence begins with a capital letter, regardless of the word or its function. Every sentence ends with a period, question mark, or exclamation point.

See also: PARAGRAPHS; PUNCTUATION

*   *   *

Slash: *SEE* **PUNCTUATION**

SEXIST WRITING

Sensitivity to the sexes is a modern problem in business writing. In the past, the default writing style was to identify all unknown people in the masculine; today, the goal is to avoid sexist writing.

1. Avoid using masculine nouns and pronouns when referring to both sexes or either sex.

Choose words that apply universally, such as *everyone, everybody, someone, somebody,* and *people.*

Sexist language:
We are counting on every man in the company.
One of the women in the department made a mistake.
You men need to attend this meeting.

Preferred language:
We are counting on everyone in the company.
Someone in the department made a mistake.
All of you need to attend this meeting.

2. Avoid using words that clearly identify the sex of the individual (unless you are referring to a particular person).

Select alternative words. An exception to this rule is when avoiding a sexist word makes a sentence awkward. The trend is toward applying sexually nonspecific terms to both sexes.

Examples:

Sex-Specific Words	*Alternatives*
mankind	people, humanity
manpower	labor force
waitress	server
chairman	chair *or* chairperson

3.   Select letter salutations to be general when the sex of the receiver is not known or when the letter is addressed to more than one person.

Examples:

Sex-Specific Words	*Alternatives*
Gentlemen:	Gentlemen and Ladies:
	Gentlemen or Ladies:
Dear Sir:	Dear Sir or Madam:

Sometimes the individual's name does not indicate whether the person is male or female. In such cases, address the letter to the individual's full name. For example, if the receiver's name is Robin Smith, address the letter, Dear Robin Smith.

4.   Avoid hybrid forms of personal pronouns and possessive adjectives.

These are distracting and unacceptable.

Examples:
s/he
his or her
he/she
(wo)man

5.   Use plurals to avoid problems of agreement.

One of the problems that arises when trying to avoid sexist writing is that of agreement.

Incorrect agreement:
Each manager should pass the message to their departments and make sure their subordinates understand it completely.

Correct but awkward agreement:

> Each manager should pass the massage to his or her
> department and make sure subordinates understand it
> completely.

This problem often can be avoided by the consistent use of plural form. Considering the example, plural is also a preferable style of expression, as this type of statement often involves generalization.

Correct agreement:

> Managers should pass the message to their departments
> and make sure their subordinates understand it
> completely.

Sometimes the plural does not work in a sentence. If this is the case, the preferred form is "he or she" or "she or he."

6. Never use the word *girl* when referring to women.

The preferred form of expression is to avoid identifying the sex of an individual.

Incorrect usage:

> Give it to the girls in the word processing department.

Correct usage:

> Give it to the people in the word processing department.

*   *   *

SIGNS AND SYMBOLS

Each industry uses its own specialized language and glossary of specific words. Several industries also employ signs and symbols to abbreviate a larger and more complex meaning. The more an industry is involved in mathematical, electrical, chemical, and other technical sciences, the more likely it is that signs and symbols will appear in the communications of the organization.

1. Publish a glossary of commonly used signs and symbols.

If an organization's personnel consist of technical and nontechnical employees (virtually always the case), improve internal communication with a published glossary, and make it available to everyone in the organization.

2. When unusual signs and symbols are used in narratives, explain them in parentheses or with a footnote.

A sign or symbol may come up only in rare cases, so some readers might not understand its meaning. Explain such symbols in parentheses if the explanation is brief and with a footnote if longer.

3. Use technical symbols in tables, charts, and graphs but not in narrative.

In text, avoid using symbols—for example, use *54 percent*, not *54%*. As a general rule, spell out the meaning of the symbol in text. However, when a symbol is used frequently, spelling it out may not make sense. For example, in financial reporting, using % may be preferable, even in text.

*   *   *

SIMILAR WORDS

Many style problems grow from the similarities in spelling between words or from the similar uses and meanings of phrases close in definition but not the same. Following are many common similar words and brief descriptions of proper use. (The explanation follows the order of the words.)

a/an:

Use prior to consonant, versus use prior to a vowel sound.

> A better way is to research first.
> An easier *method* should be found.

accept/except:

The verb "to receive," versus the preposition meaning "excluding."

> Will you accept and sign for this delivery?
> All quarters were profitable except the second.

ad/add:

An abbreviation for "advertisement," versus a mathematical function.

> Place the ad in all daily papers.
> Add the columns to find the total.

adapt/adept:

To adjust, versus skillful.

> Let's adapt our procedures so they will work.
> They are adept at interpreting financial statements.

adverse/averse:

Unfavorable, versus having a distaste:

> The adverse comments led us to decline the offer.
> We were averse to the expensive proposal.

advice/advise:

A noun meaning "suggestion," versus a verb meaning "to rec-ommend."

> Our advice was to increase the budget.
> I advise you to make a written report to personnel.

affect/effect:

A verb meaning "to influence," versus a noun meaning "result, outcome, or consequence."

> Customer attitude will affect buying habits.
> The effect of the study has been to discourage risk.

agree to/agree with:

To give one's consent, versus to have an understanding.

> We will agree to a one-month extension.
> I agree with you about the budget problems.

all ready/already:

Reference to complete readiness or to plural readiness, versus past action.

> The attendees were all ready and in the room.
> We already balanced the accounts.

all right/alright:

Correct form, versus informal, incorrect usage. Use *all right*, and avoid usage of *alright*.

all together/altogether:

In unison, versus completely.

> The inventory was finally placed all together.
> It proved altogether too difficult to balance.

allusion/delusion/illusion:

A reference to something, versus a false belief or idea, versus a mistaken impression.

> We made an allusion to problems faced by employees.
> The belief in creating profits by thinking about them is, in
>   our opinion, a delusion.
> He had the illusion there was no problem whatsoever.

alternate/alternative:

Taking place in turns, versus a choice between two or more.

> The job was made to alternate departments each month.
> The alternative was equally unacceptable.

although/though:

Used for the same references, with *although* having more emphasis:

> We exceeded expectations, although that trend should
>   not be expected to continue.
> The company had begun operating in the black though
>   the CEO had not made a formal announcement.

among/between:

Several choices, versus usually only two (although *between* often is used for more than two).

> The eleven employees decided among themselves.
> It came down to a choice between Sue and David.

amount/number:

Reference to uncountable quantities, versus reference to countable quantities.

> We will require a large amount of sand to fill this hole.
> A significant number of customers responded.

anyone/any one:

Anybody or any person, versus any specific, singular person or thing.

> Anyone who arrives early will get the best chair.
> The job may be performed by any one of you.

anyway/any way:

Even so or in any event, versus a reference to options for action.

> We were not planning to attend anyway.
> Any way it can be achieved will be appreciated.

appraise/apprise:

An estimate of value, versus providing of information.

> The headquarters building will be appraised in
>   anticipation of refinancing.
> Please apprise us of the situation as it develops.

around/round:

An approximation or loose reference to a location, versus a shape.

> The total is around a half million.
> The meeting room's table is round.

as/like:

A subordinating conjunction, versus a preposition.

> We stopped and talked as the meeting broke up.
> We laughed like children.

ascent/assent:

To rise, versus to agree.

> Our average profit by division is on the ascent.
> Will you assent to an audit?

assure/ensure/insure:

All three words refer to promises or guarantees; however, *assure* refers to people while *ensure* tends to refer obliquely to less personal promises; *insure* is a financial term related to the idea of insurance.

> I can assure you the task will be done on time.
> The safeguards ensure compliance with all rules.
> We have to insure our building against risk of loss.

bazaar/bizarre:

a marketplace, versus odd or strange.

> The ancient place for exchange was the bazaar.
> His behavior was bizarre during the interview.

beside/besides:

Next to, versus in addition to.

> He sat beside me during the seminar.
> We made a profit last year; besides, our future costs are
>   anticipated to fall.

biannually/biennially:

Twice per year, versus every two years.

> The review is held biannually, in January and July.
> We will meet biennally, in odd-numbered years.

billed/build:

Sent an invoice or statement, versus construct.

> We bill the customers on the tenth of each month.
> We will build new offices rather than lease space.

bimonthly/semimonthly:

Every other month, versus twice per month.

> We meet bimonthly, in even-numbered months.
> The review meeting is held semimonthly, on the second
>   and fourth Tuesday.

bloc/block:

A coalition, versus a solid mass or unit.

> We formed with our competitors as a lobbying bloc.
> The stock price is lower when transacted as a block.

board/bored:

A body (or piece of wood), versus a tired or wearied state.

> The board of directors meeting takes place next week.
> A board is loose in our fence.
> I am bored with the repetitive tasks of my job.

breath/breathe/breadth:

A small amount of air, versus the act of respirating, versus width.

> I need to go outside for a breath of air.

It's so stuffy I can't breathe in here.
The length isn't the problem; it's the breadth.

bring/take:

Reference to something being brought to the speaker, versus something being moved away.

Bring me your books.
Take these books when you leave.

by/buy/bye:

A preposition, versus the act of purchasing, versus a secondary reference or parting comment.

We go by the book here.
The company wants to buy out its competitor.
Good-bye.

can/may:

Ability, versus permission (with some overlap).

We can complete the report on time.
You may take the afternoon off.

canvas/canvass:

A durable cloth, versus the conducting of a survey or poll.

The tents were a bleached canvas.
We canvassed customers in the area.

capital/capitol:

The central site (or investment, or upper-case lettering), versus a government building.

Washington is the capital of the United States.
Businesses have invested a large amount of capital.

The first word of the sentence begins with a capital letter.
The capitol is recognized by its large dome.

cash/cache:

Money, versus a secret hiding place.

We do not accept cash by mail.
Think of the reserve account as a cache for corporate-level
emergencies.

cast/caste:

A collection of players, versus a societal class.

The marketing cast consists of a strong executive and
aggressive, knowledgeable field managers.
Our lower-level employees often think they are viewed as
a lower caste.

casual/causal:

Informal, versus a reason for an event.

We viewed the problem with casual unawareness.
The causal data were overlooked by the method of
questioning.

cede/seed:

To give to another, versus the beginning or source.

We will cede those accounts to the competing marketing
group.
The seed of our troubles was the vague agreement itself.

censor/censure:

To suppress material, versus to criticize:

Please censor your personal opinions from this report.

We were censured by the regulatory agency.

cite/sight/site:

A quotation, versus reference to vision, versus a place or location.

Please cite your source for that information.
Profitability is not yet in sight for the division.
This corner is the site for our new offices.

coarse/course:

Rough, versus a path or method.

The previous marketing methods were perceived as being too coarse.
We have selected our course carefully.

collision/collusion:

A colliding or conflict, versus a conspiracy.

The two managers had a personality collision that needed immediate resolution.
The embezzlement was achieved in a way that required collusion.

compare to/compare with:

Similarity, versus to check or observe similarities.

Let's compare last year's numbers to this year's.
Please don't compare our results with those of dissimilar industries.

complement/compliment:

The act of finishing or adding to, versus praise or acknowledgment.

The revisions complement the budget process.
The letter was a compliment for the work we did.

comprehensible/comprehensive:

So that it can be understood, versus extensive.

> Finally we have a version of the report that is
> comprehensible enough for nontechnicians to read.
> I particularly admired the comprehensive analysis of every
> option available.

comprise/compose:

To include, versus to create.

> The department comprises three sections.
> We need to compose a cover letter for the report.

confidant/confident:

One with whom sensitive information can be entrusted, versus
a self-assured attitude.

> I consider you a confidant, or I wouldn't tell you any of
> this.
> I am confident my numbers are accurate.

conscience/conscious:

A moral standard, versus being awake or aware.

> Our conscience would bother us.
> We are conscious of the way you feel.

continual/continuous:

Repeating or occurring frequently, versus ongoing without inter-
ruption.

> We suffer continual unfavorable variances in this account.
> The budget review process is a continuous job.

controller/comptroller:

A financial officer of a company, versus a public official.

> The company's controller issued a balance sheet.
> The comptroller of the currency issued a press release.

council/counsel/consul:

An organized group of people, versus the verb *to give advice* or the noun meaning "attorney," versus a foreign government's spokesperson.

> The council advised the company to abandon the plan.
> Please counsel us as to the best course to take.
> We asked our counsel for an opinion.
> The British consul will visit our main office.

councilor/counselor:

A member of an organized group, versus an attorney or other adviser.

> The councilors met at the usual time.
> Our corporate counselor is preparing a brief.

credible/creditable/credulous:

Believable and trustworthy, versus admirable, versus gullible.

> After the proposed changes, the budget was viewed as a credible document.
> We were pleased that the report offered a creditable alternative to the problem.
> We were credulous to hire that individual without verifying his claimed background.

credit/accredit:

A noun for one side of an accounting entry or a verb to post benefit, versus certification or acknowledgment.

> The debit was offset by an equal credit.
> I will credit the payment to your account.
> He is an accredited professional.

criteria/criterion:

Plural, versus singular.

> These criteria have to be observed.
> Accuracy is the only criterion.

data/datum:

Plural, versus singular (however, *data* often is used incorrectly used for both, while *datum* is rarely used).

> Those data are correct.
> The datum is only one piece of the story.

definite/definitive:

Certain, versus conclusive.

> There is a definite trend toward profitability.
> This is the definitive procedure.

depositary/depository:

A person entrusted with funds, versus the place where funds are left.

> He is the depositary for cash on hand.
> The corner bank serves as depository for us.

deprecate/depreciate:

To disapprove, versus to decline in value.

> The report deprecated the motives and reputation of the
>   company and the industry.
> The machinery is worthless due to functional depreciation.

descent/dissent:

A downward movement, versus disagreement.

> Our volume continues its quarterly descent.
> Voices of dissent within the company are not always
> productive.

deserve/disserve:

To be worthy, versus to serve poorly.

> The department deserves recognition for its work.
> We have been disserved by the unfair criticism.

detract/distract:

To take away from, versus to draw attention away from.

> The introduction of personal views detracts from the main
> argument.
> Our employees were distracted by the noise outside.

device/devise:

A tool or utility, versus a verb meaning "to formulate."

> The computer is an essential device for inventory control.
> We need to devise a method for faster turnaround time.

differ from/differ with:

To be dissimilar, versus to disagree.

> We differ from other companies in that our product
> cannot be duplicated.
> We differ with one another about how to proceed.

disassemble/dissemble:

To undo or take apart, versus to mask.

> The machine has to be disassembled and fixed.

The report dissembles the real problem.

disburse/disperse:

To pay out, versus to scatter.

> The payroll department disburses checks on Friday.
> As the meeting broke up, attendees dispersed.

discreet/discrete:

Reference to tact or caution, versus individual or unique:

> She was discreet in checking references.
> The manufacturing process ensures that every product is discrete.

disinterested/uninterested:

Without bias, versus lacking in concern or interest:

> The arbitrator must be a disinterested party.
> Because the decision will not affect us, we are completely uninterested.

egoism/egotism:

Thought of one's self, versus speaking of one's self.

> His egoism prevented his understanding of others.
> The speech was characterized by egotism.

elicit/illicit:

To draw out, versus improper or illegal.

> We intend to elicit opinions on the issue.
> This action was illicit and should not be repeated.

emigrate/immigrate:

To go to another place, versus to come into this place.

> Our product has emigrated to Europe.
> The CEO immigrated from England.

eminent/imminent:

With prestige, versus pending.

> The keynote speaker was an eminent lecturer.
> The collapse of this stock price, in our opinion, is
> imminent.

envelop/envelope:

To enclose, versus a wrapper.

> Our market strategy is to envelop the whole region.
> Please place the report in a sealed envelope.

erasable/irascible:

Able to be erased, versus hot-tempered.

> They used erasable paper, which was a mistake.
> The manager is known for his irascible personality.

especial/special:

Extraordinary and exceptional, versus an exception.

> This was an especial task, and it was done well.
> There is a special reason for my request.

estop/estoppel/stop:

To bar under law, versus a bar due to a previous action, versus
to cease.

The law may estop you from proceeding without first
having a court test.
The standard of collateral estoppel prevents us from trying
this case again.
We were ordered to stop at once.

exercise/exorcise:

To take action, versus to force away.

We will exercise our legal rights.
The poor attitude must be exorcised from the ranks.

explicit/implicit:

Defined without doubt, versus implied or alluded to.

I was quite explicit so there can be no doubt.
The lack of response was taken as implicit agreement.

extant/extent:

Still in existence, versus a reference to degrees.

A small degree of competition is extant in virtually all
regions.
To what extent do we want to commit resources to
investigating even the smallest variance?

facetious/factious/factitious/fictitious:

Humorous or witty, versus promoting of conflict, versus fake or
ungenuine, versus false.

His facetious remarks were appreciated.
The factious attitude only isolated the department from the
rest of the division.
The study, because it manipulated data, has to be viewed
as factitious.
The claim is provably fictitious, and we have ample data
showing that the opposite is true.

faint/feint:

In a weakened state, versus a ploy or deception.

> I felt faint in the stuffy room.
> The announcement was a feint designed to force our hand.

farther/further:

References to distance, versus nongeographic descriptions such as more advanced or more developed.

> New York is farther from here than Trenton.
> Upon further consideration, the offer was rejected.
> We are further along on the task than the others.

fewer/less:

Things that can be counted, versus unknown quantities.

> Fewer employees are required in that department.
> That is less important at this point.

first/firstly:

Proper form, versus jargon. With all listings by number, avoid -ly endings. Use *first, second, third,* and so forth.

flare/flair:

A flaming outward, versus ability.

> The new product has flared in the market.
> She demonstrated a particular flair for the job.

for/fore/four:

A preposition, versus in the front, versus a numeral.

> This report was prepared for you.

We are in the fore among our competitors.
We report four times per year.

forgo/forego:

To do without, versus to precede.

We will have to forgo our company picnic this year.
The foregoing section of this report demonstrated this.

forward/foreword:

Near the front or moving toward the front, versus an introductory section.

Move forward to the front of the room.
I was asked to write the foreword to the report.

good/well:

An adjective, versus an adverb or an adjective describing health.

I have a good feeling about this project.
It was a job well done.
He did not feel well and left the office early.

guarantee/guaranty:

Noun to warrant or verb to provide warranty, versus a financial security or policy.

The guarantee was enforceable in court.
Can you guarantee the accuracy of these numbers?
The guaranty bond is with our attorney.

healthful/healthy:

Beneficial to health, versus being in good health.

Because they buy and use our healthful products, our
    customers are healthy.

hypercritical/hypocritical:

Overly critical, versus pretentious and smug.

> We believe that management is hypercritical when it comes to our reports.
>
> The board members ignored our advice, demonstrating a hypocritical belief that they did not need us.

if/whether:

Statement of a condition, versus alternatives.

> We will present the information only if we are allowed to attend the full meeting.
>
> I don't know yet whether to ask.

imply/infer:

To make a suggestion, versus to derive as a conclusion.

> While offering no proof, the speaker seemed to imply that such budgetary systems never work.
>
> I infer from your comments that you are not available to help with this project.

in/into:

Location or status, versus change of condition or place.

> We are in New York now.
> Our company is in trouble financially.
> We moved into new offices last month.
> Let's get into the project.

incidence/incidents:

An occurrence or rate of occurrence, versus a series of occurrences or events.

> The incidence of complaint is on the decline.
> There was a high incidence of absenteeism just before the holiday.
> There have been fewer incidents this past year.

incredible/incredulous:

Unbelievable, versus unbelieving.

> The report was incredible.
> We are incredulous at what the report claims.

ingenious/ingenuous:

Clear or brilliant, versus candid and frank.

> The solution was ingenious in its simplicity.
> We simply provided the most ingenuous arguments.

insight/incite:

Vision or understanding, versus instigation.

> The discussion gave me great insight into your concerns.
> Do not attempt to incite our competitors.

insoluble/insolvable/insolvent:

Unable to be dissolved, versus the inability to explain, versus the inability to pay debts.

> The material is insoluble, making it appropriate for its
>   intended use.
> The problem appears insolvable at this level.
> The company has been declared insolvent.

instance/instants:

Example or event, versus moments.

> In this instance, the tests all failed.
> We were in agreement for a few instants.

intelligent/intelligible:

Having cognitive ability, versus understandable.

> Our leaders have demonstrated their intelligence.

The technical report, although complex, was completely intelligible.

interstate/intrastate:

Between more than one state, versus within one state only.

We are subject to federal rules because our markets operate on an interstate basis.
We are restricted to only intrastate activity under terms of the charter.

irregardless/regardless:

The proper word is always *regardless,* which means the same as *nonetheless.* Avoid use of the improper form, *irregardless.*

its/it's:

A possessive form of the pronoun, versus a contraction for *it is.*

We read the entire report, except its supplementary attachments.
It's clear to us that changes are required.

lain and lay/lie:

Forms of the verb *lie* (meaning "to recline horizontally"); *lie* by itself is a noun or verb meaning "to prevaricate."

Obsolete supplies had lain in the warehouse for over a year.
The store lay on the main traffic route.
The building lies at the corner of Main and Broadway.
A lie is never acceptable. [noun]
Do not lie to others. [verb]

last/latest:

Final, versus most recent.

The last store closed this month.

This is only the latest in a series of reports.

later/latter:

A comparative form of *late,* versus reference to the second of two possibilities:

> The decision will be made later.
> Of Detroit or Chicago as a convention site, we prefer the latter.

learn/teach:

Acquiring information, versus giving information to others.

> We are trying to learn the new procedures.
> Let me teach you how to use this equipment.

lend/loan:

A verb only, versus a noun or a verb.

> We hope the bank will lend capital to our company.
> We want to finance our expansion with a bank loan.
> Are you willing to loan us the money?

liable/libel/likely:

Responsible, versus a complaint in law or a written statement defamatory to another, versus plausibly.

> We are liable for statements made by employees.
> A libel suit was filed against the author.
> You are likely to be promoted for your work.

lightening/lightning:

To lighten in weight or responsibility, versus a natural event.

> We are lightening our departmental workload.
> The building was struck by lightning.

literal/littoral:

Exactly, versus reference to shoreline legal issues.

> This is a literal interpretation of the rules.
> Our contract for acquisition of property by the water
> included a discussion of our littoral rights.

loose/lose:

Unfastened or unsecured, versus to misplace or part with.

> The handle on my door is loose.
> That is a loose interpretation of the rule.
> I always lose my glasses.
> We will lose money this year.

maybe/may be:

An adverb meaning "perhaps," versus a verb meaning "possibly."

> Maybe we will break for an early lunch.
> The outcome may be beyond our control.

media/medium:

Plural, versus singular.

> The media are interested in this story.
> What is the best medium for our news release?

metal/mettle:

A solid substance, versus courage or resolve.

> I ordered a metal desk rather than one of wood.
> It required mettle to confront your manager.

modal/model:

Of a mode, versus a prototype or style.

> What is the modal payment: monthly or quarterly?
> This is a model cost control plan.

moral/morale:

Ethical conduct, versus mood or state of mind.

> Admitting the flaw is the only moral thing to do.
> Due to poor communication, morale is very low.

motif/motive:

A theme, versus a reason for something's pattern.

> We market this product with the "tasty" motif.
> What is the motive for that behavior?

needed/needful/needy:

Required or wanted, versus necessary or essential, versus in need.

> We needed the report last week.
> The proper treatment of customers is needful to our long-
> term success.
> The charitable fund-raiser will help the needy.

observance/observation:

Compliance, versus the act of watching and learning.

> In observance of the law, the reports will be filed.
> My observation was that the work was done correctly.

OK/O.K./Okay:

All forms of the same expression meaning "all right." The full spelling is preferred in formal documents; the abbreviation, with or without periods, is acceptable in internal memos or notes.

oral/verbal:

The act of speaking, versus of words or by word of mouth.

> We entered into an oral contract.
> The subtle meaning was lost in the verbal translation.

past/passed:

Time gone by, versus gone beyond or successfully completed.

> That's what we did in the past.
> The practice has passed with the advent of computers.
> I passed the test.

peak/peek/pique:

The top, versus a glance, versus to provoke.

> The chart shows that profits peaked last year.
> Let me have an advance peek at the report.
> Don't pique him into a confrontation.

percent/percentage:

The number of segments out of 100, versus the less specific relationship between a value and 100:

> Only 35 percent of all customers returned.
> A relatively small percentage of customers returned.

perpetrate/perpetuate:

To cause or be guilty of, versus to keep something going.

> The offense was perpetrated by an unnamed person.

The problem is perpetuated by continued poor fiscal policies.

persecute/prosecute:

To oppress or harass, versus to sue or complain under the law.

Do not persecute me for my opinions.
The attorney general said he would prosecute.

personal/personnel:

Individually, versus the staff or department engaged in employment matters.

This is a personal problem between the employees.
Send a copy to the personnel department.

perspective/prospective:

Views or belief in balance, versus anticipated status.

Our perspective changed with more information.
All prospective customers want to be asked.

phenomena/phenomenon:

Plural, versus singular.

These phenomena are unpredictable.
The phenomenon was undoubtedly a one-time event.

portion/proportion:

A part or to divide into parts, versus relationships or ratio segments.

We received only a portion of the market share.
The work will be portioned among the staff.
The greater proportion of funds is spent in marketing and related efforts.

practical/practicable:

Proven and realistic, versus able to be achieved. The words are used interchangeably. The recommended style decision is to use the simpler form, *practical,* for both meanings.

precede/proceed:

To come before, versus to go ahead.

> On the balance sheet, assets precede liabilities.
> Let's proceed with the inventory audit.

precedence/precedents:

Singular noun meaning "priority," versus plural noun meaning a "case or example."

> Cost controls take precedence over other actions.
> We sought out precedents to establish the legality of our position.

predicate/predict:

To base upon, versus to forecast.

> Our assumptions are predicated on experience.
> We predict a twofold increase in sales volume.

prescribe/proscribe:

To suggest or order, versus to prohibit.

> We prescribe tighter cost and expense controls.
> Payments without proper authorization are proscribed by our internal controls.

pretend/portend:

To make believe or base actions on role playing, versus to fore-shadow or signal in advance.

Let's pretend we're in charge of making the final
  decisions.
This financial statement portends serious trouble.

principal/principle:

Noun meaning "head person" or adjective meaning "primary"
or "leading," versus a standard or belief.

The principal of the school gave a keynote speech.
The principal reasons are listed in the report.
The principles of good accounting must be applied.

provided/providing:

Conditional, versus to furnish.

We will agree provided we are granted a concession.
Our department will be providing the information.

quiet/quit/quite:

With less noise, versus to give up, versus considerably.

We need quiet in order to concentrate.
The manager quit yesterday.
This is quite an improvement.

quotation/quote:

A noun referring to a verbatim use of words, versus the verb *to
repeat* (also used informally as an abbreviated form of *quotation).*

The quotation was used to make the point.
Please don't quote me.
The quote came from an old book. [informal]

raise/rise:

To uplift or increase, versus to go up.

> We were all given a raise.
> Don't raise our expectations.
> The elevator began to rise.
> I hope to rise in the organization.

real/really:

Adjective, versus adverb.

> The real reasons are unknown to us.
> We are really going to get approval this time.

register/registrar/registry:

A record, versus an officer in charge of keeping records, versus the place where the register is maintained.

> This is the official register of daily receipts.
> The registrar is responsible for recording every payment
>   that comes through the mail.
> The registry is also called the cashier's cage.

respectfully/respectively:

In a courteous or considerate manner, versus in the indicated order.

> We respectfully asked for a meeting.
> Net profits during the first, second, and third quarters
>   were 8, 6, and 7 percent, respectively.

right/rite/write/wright:

Correctness or a legal protection, versus a ceremony, versus to set words to paper, versus a worker skilled in a task.

We had the right to speak out.
The rite involved sitting and kneeling for hours.
We will write our ideas in a report.
The playwright produced his new three-act play.

root/route:

The source or a mathematical value, versus a roadway or course.

The root of our problem is poor internal control.
The square root of 64 is 8.
We selected the shortest driving route.

scrip/script:

A form of promissory note, versus a scenario or (in law) an original document.

The emergency management team handed out scrip to
    their workers.
The meeting was obviously scripted in advance.

set/sit:

To put, versus to be seated.

I want to set the record straight.
Please sit down.

shall/will:

Obligatory action or part of a question (sometimes used interchangeably with *should*), versus a simple future verb (the word *shall*, when used in legal documents, indicates mandatory actions rather than optional).

The corporation shall provide written notice within three
    weeks of such changes.
Shall we meet on Tuesday?
We will meet on Tuesday.

some time/sometime/sometimes:

A period of identified time, versus an indefinite time or occasional role, versus occasionally.

> We stopped using that procedure some time ago.
> We will get around to a file audit sometime.
> Our sometime master of ceremonies is actually a clerk in
>   the legal research department.
> We sometimes meet for lunch.

stationary/stationery:

Remaining in one spot, versus paper and related writing supplies.

> Our profitability has been stationary for four years.
> Our stationery supplies are running low.

statue/statute:

A model or piece or art, versus a law.

> The statue in the courtyard is of our founder.
> We must operate under restrictions of the statute.

straight/strait:

In a direct line or correctly, versus a narrow opening.

> I used a ruler to draw a straight line.
> We were cautioned to keep the files straight.
> The bay narrowed into a strait.

summon/summons:

A verb to call or order to appear, versus a noun representing an order.

> I was summoned to the manager's office.
> The summons was addressed to me.

sure and/sure to:

Improper form, versus intended form.

> Be sure and call. [improper]
> Be sure to call. [proper]

sustenance/subsistence:

The basic necessities for life, versus expenses or maintenance.

> Everyone's budget priority is sustenance for self and for
> family.
> I was provided a meager subsistence allowance while out
> of town.

than/then:

A word of comparison, versus an adverb denoting time.

> This year's budget turned out to be more accurate than
> last year's.
> We met in the lobby and then went to lunch.

their/there/they're:

A possessive adjective, versus an indication of a place, versus a
contraction of *they are.*

> Employees balanced their own accounts.
> The records are filed over there.
> They're attending a field survey today.

through/threw:

From one end to the other or passing within or done with, versus
past tense of *throw.*

> We went through the report from start to finish.
> The new freeway passed right through town.
> I am through with these arguments.
> We threw the whole thing out.

to/too/two:

A preposition, versus a word meaning "also" or an adverb indicating excess, versus the numeral:

> We went to the executive office.
> My friend, too, works here.
> It was too hot to work.
> We had two additional staff members available.

toward/towards:

The former is preferred, although both have the same meaning and usage.

track/tract:

A path or course, versus a parcel of land.

> The proper track is described in our procedures.
> The company purchased a tract for its new building.

transmission/transmittal:

Sending a message without physical substance, versus sending a message with substance.

> The transmission came in by fax today.
> The letter was accompanied by a transmittal.

try and/try to:

Improper, versus proper form.

> Try and remember. [improper]
> Try to remember. [proper]

until/till:

Until is more formal than *till*, although both are acceptable.

urban/urbane:

Of a city, versus polished.

> Our urban stores tend to have higher profits.
> His urbane tone indicated that he was well educated.

venerable/vulnerable:

Respected due to age, versus easily hurt.

> The venerable chairman approached the podium.
> You seem vulnerable to even the slightest criticism.

vindicative/vindictive:

Clearing suspicions, versus seeking revenge.

> This information is vindicative for those we suspected.
> Rather than hearing our ideas as constructive criticism,
> they were vindictive and angry.

wait for/wait on:

To remain ready, versus to serve.

> We are waiting for the report.
> The server should be here to wait on us.

waive/wave:

To give up a right, versus a hand motion.

> We hereby wave our right to a hearing.
> Wave to the audience as you leave the stage.

weather/whether:

Natural conditions, versus an alternative.

> Let's hope the weather permits an outside event.
> We have to decide whether to say yes or no.

which/who:

Reference to objects, versus reference to people.

> Which department do you work in?
> Who is your supervisor?

who's/whose:

A contraction of *who is,* versus the possessive form of *who.*

> Who's attending this summer's retreat?
> Whose desk is this?

wont/won't:

Accustomed versus a contraction for *will not.*

> They are wont to repeat themselves.
> We won't allow this to happen.

your/you're:

The possessive of *you,* versus a contraction for *you are.*

> Your report was well received.
> You're expected to speak at the task force meeting.

*   *   *

SINGULAR AND PLURAL

The method for formation of a plural depends on the noun or pronoun. Many nouns do not follow a regular pattern, and their plural forms have to be memorized or learned through familiarity. The greatest problem for those unfamiliar with the rules is that of inconsistency. For each rule, there may be a lengthy list of exceptions.

1. Form most plurals by adding *s* to the singular form.

The most common rule is to add *s* to the singular form of the noun. The word's spelling is not altered at all.

Examples:

Singular	Plural
employee	employees
manager	managers
budget	budgets

2. For nouns ending in a *y* preceded by a consonant, drop the *y* and replace it with *ies* to form a plural.

Examples:

Singular	Plural
company	companies
inventory	inventories

When nouns end in a *y* that is preceded by a vowel, plurals are formed by adding an *s*.

Examples:

Singular	Plural
Monday	Mondays
Friday	Fridays
day	days
play	plays

3. Add -*es* to form plurals for some nouns ending in consonants.

Nouns ending in consonants or with an *o* often require an -*es* ending to form the plural. Consult a dictionary for specific instances.

Examples:

Singular	Plural
echo	echoes
veto	vetoes

4. Be aware of unusual plural formations.

Some words ending in *s* are made into plurals by changing the preceding letter; such a change usually involves turning an *i* into an *e*.

Examples:

Singular	Plural
analysis	analyses
thesis	theses
axis	axes

Technical terms ending in *a* often require the addition of the letter *e* to form a plural. Some Latin terms are made plural by dropping the singular ending and replacing it with an *a*.

Examples:

Singular	Plural
larva	larvae
seta	setae
addendum	addenda

Nouns often change in form to convert to plural. This is the most troublesome aspect of plurals because there are no consistent rules.

Examples:

Singular	Plural
matrix	matrices
nucleus	nuclei
radius	radii
child	children

5. Be aware of the irregular plural forms for pronouns.

Pronouns tend to be very irregular when converted to plural form, with no pattern or consistency.

Examples:

Singular	Plural
I	we
me	us
he, she, it	they

	Singular	Plural
	him, her, it	them
	you	you

6. Turn some compound terms into plural form by adding an *s* to the key word rather than to the final word.

Examples:

Singular	Plural
attorney at law	attorneys at law
grant in aid	grants in aid
chief of staff	chiefs of staff

7. Do not confuse plurals with possessive form.

The possessive usually involves the addition of an *s* with an apostrophe. The apostrophe follows the existing *s* ending when the singular form ends in *s* or when the noun is already a plural.

Examples:

Noun	Plural	Possessive
man	men	man's, men's
woman	women	woman's, women's
employee	employees	employee's, employees'

8. If it can be done without creating confusion, add an *s* without an apostrophe to form plurals for many abbreviations and acronyms.

Examples:

Singular	Plural
COD	CODs
OK	OKs
SOP	SOPs
Ph.D.	Ph.D.'s
M.B.A.	M.B.A.'s

See also: AGREEMENT; POSSESSIVES

*   *   *

Spacing

Decisions concerning spacing in documents affect the ability of a reader to comprehend information, degrees of acceptance or resistance even to reading the material, and the opinion the reader will have of the individual writer and of the company. Readers need to have text broken up with "white space"—areas with nothing on them that emphasize or offset text, tables, and graphics.

1. Select spacing of margins depending on the nature of the document.

As a general rule, all letters, reports, proposals, and other formal documents should leave at least 1 inch on the left, right, top, and bottom of every page. Some people prefer up to 1½ inches. For letters written on company letterhead, the arrangement of pre-printed material might determine the actual spacing. If pre-printed matter appears at the bottom of the page, measure the desired distance from the top of the printed matter rather than from the page edge.

For reports and other documents exceeding one page, the margin decisions should be consistent throughout the entire document.

2. Single- or double-space the text depending on the type of document.

Business letters are normally single-spaced; reports, proposals, procedures manuals, and training material tend to be double-spaced for ease of reading. More white space usually means that readers are more willing to read a greater amount of material. If a letter is single-spaced, leave a double space between paragraphs and extend all margins to allow greater white space.

3. Allow space around tables and charts.

Graphics usually appear in reports or proposals, which should be double-spaced. If the chart or graph appears on a page by itself, it should be arranged with previously determined margin size kept consistent. If the graphic or table appears above or below the text or in the middle of a page, leave three or four spaces between the text and the graphic. Do not break up a table between two pages unless it is more than one page long. In this case, try to insert it on facing pages.

4. Space generously on title pages and for heads and subheads.

Make sure that, even with other emphasis, the break in thought and section is obvious. At the end of one section, leave at least four spaces (up to six if single-spaced) before listing the next subheading. Leave an extra space (or two if single-spaced) between the subhead and the beginning of the first paragraph in that section.

5. Use spacing to plan the size of documents.

If you need to extend the size of a document, allowing more white space is an acceptable method, as long as such movement of text is not excessive.

6. Follow punctuation guidelines.

The following rules are general and refer to most business documents. However, if you are preparing a manuscript for publication, even within your own organization, be sure to obtain precise guidelines prior to adopting spacing and punctuation rules. (For the purpose of this section, a "space" refers to the space bar on the keyboard rather than an index space on the page.)

- Any punctuation ending a sentence should be followed by two spaces; a sentence interrupted by a colon should also be followed by a double space.
- Semicolons in mid-sentence should be placed after the previous word without a space and should be followed with a single space.
- When printing dashes or hyphens, do not leave space on either side.
- Commas are always placed at the end of a word without a space, and followed by a single space.
- Leave a space on either side of ellipses and spaces between the three periods.
- Leave a single space on the outside of parentheses and brackets in text. Include no spaces on the inside before beginning enclosed narratives or after ending them.

* * *

SPELLING

The convenient access to word processing spell-check programs helps avoid the common spelling problems in English. Because so many words represent exceptions to general rules, there are only a few useful rules worth remembering. A listing of commonly misspelled words will help avoid common problems; a comprehensive listing is included at the end of this section.

1. Use automated programs to find and fix spelling errors, including typographical errors.

Virtually all word processors include a key stroke that will check the spelling of all words in a document. Most include a function to suggest alternatives and to correct misspelled words. This quick and convenient feature should be used for *all* documents.

2. No automated program can find a correctly spelled typographical error.

If *am* is typed instead of *an*, a spell-checker will not find the error. It is still necessary to read through a document carefully. The advantage of a spell-checker program is that it finds errors the writer might not realize have been made.

3. Improve spelling by avoiding common problems.

Even a poor speller can eliminate common problems by memorizing a list of commonly misspelled words and by avoiding unnecessarily complex word forms. Most people have chronic problems with a very limited list of words they do not spell correctly. Make a list of such words, and check the list each time you use these words.

A good vocabulary does not necessitate long or difficult-to-spell words. Avoid complex words when shorter, more direct words have the same meaning. A simplified common vocabulary often translates to a clearer, more concise style and better communication.

4. Learn a few general spelling rules to improve overall spelling ability.

These rules include:

- Put *i* before *e* except after *c* (e.g., *conceit, receive, deceive, perceive*).
- When adding a suffix to a word ending in *y*, change the *y* to an *i*. When adding *-ing*, keep the *y* (e.g., *try, tries, trying*). However, when the *y* is preceded by a vowel, the change to *i* does not always apply (e.g., *play, plays; betray, betrays*).
- When a word ends in a consonant, the consonant is often

doubled when adding *-ed* or *-ing* (e.g., *stop, stopped, stop-ping; occur, occurred, occurring*).

5. Don't be ashamed to look words up in a dictionary!

Many business writers compile a list of their own personal spelling demons.

6. Study and master this list of commonly misspelled words.

absence	affect	appraise
absorb	affidavit	appreciable
absorption	aggravate	apprise
academic	aggression	appropriate
acceptable	aging	approximate
accessible	aisle	aquatic
accidentally	alignment	arbitrary
accommodate	alleged	architect
accompanied	already	argument
accumulate	although	arising
accuracy	altogether	arithmetic
accustomed	amateur	around
achievement	amortize	arrangement
acknowledgment	analogous	ascend
acoustic	analysis	asinine
acquaintance	analyze	assistance
acquiesce	announcement	association
acquire	annual	athletic
acquisition	anomalous	attendance
acreage	anonymous	attorney
across	answer	audience
actually	apology	autumn
adapter	appalled	auxiliary
adjacent	apparatus	awkward
advantageous	apparent	bachelor
aegis	appearance	bankruptcy

basically
beginning
belief
believe
beneficial
benefited
biased
boundary
breakfast
breathe
brethren
brilliant
brochure
buoyant
bureaucracy
business
cafeteria
caffeine
calendar
caliber
campaign
cancellation
candidate
candor
canvass
caret
carriage
category
cemetery
census
challenge
changeable
channel
characteristic
chauffeur
choose
chosen
chronological
coarsely
coincidence

collateral
college
colossal
column
commitment
committee
comparison
competent
competition
complement
complete
concede
conceited
conceive
condemn
conference
confidant
connoisseur
conqueror
conscience
conscientious
conscious
consensus
consistent
continuous
controlled
controversial
convenience
coolly
council
counselor
courteous
criticism
curiosity
cynical
dealt
debtor
deceive
decision
deductible

defendant
defense
deficit
definitely
dependent
descendant
describe
description
desert
desirable
despair
desperate
despicable
detrimental
development
dictionary
difference
dignitary
dilemma
disagree
disappear
disappoint
disapprove
disastrous
discipline
discussion
disease
dissatisfied
dissimilar
distill
distinct
divide
doctrinaire
dossier
dying
ecstasy
effect
efficient
either
elaborately

elicit
eligible
eliminate
embarrass
eminent
emphasize
empty
enroll
ensure
entirely
entrepreneur
enumerate
envelop
environment
equipment
equivalent
escrow
especially
exaggerate
exceed
excellent
exercise
exhaust
exhibition
exhilarate
existence
exonerate
exorbitant
experience
explanation
extension
extraordinary
extremely
eyeing
facsimile
familiar
fantasy
fascinate
favorite
fiery

finally
financially
flammable
fluorescent
forbade
foreign
foresee
forfeit
forthright
friend
fulfill
gauge
generally
glamour
gnawing
government
grammar
grateful
gray
grievous
gruesome
guarantee
guardian
guerrilla
guidance
harass
height
hemorrhage
heroes
heterogeneous
hindrance
humane
humorous
hurriedly
hygiene
hypocrisy
ideally
idiosyncrasy
ignorant
illicit

illiterate
illogical
imaginary
immediately
immensely
impasse
inasmuch
incalculable
incidentally
incredible
indefinitely
independent
indispensable
inequity
inevitable
infinite
influential
initiative
innocuous
innovation
innuendo
inoculate
insistence
insurance
integrate
intelligent
intercede
interested
interference
interim
interrupt
involvement
irrelevant
irresistible
irritated
itinerary
jealousy
jeopardy
jewelry
judgment

knowledge
labeled
laboratory
latter
ledger
legitimate
leisure
length
lenient
liable
liaison
library
license
lien
lieutenant
lightning
likable
likelihood
liquefy
literature
logistics
loneliness
loose
luxury
lying
magazine
magnificent
maintenance
manageable
maneuver
mantle
marriage
material
mathematics
meant
medieval
mediocre
memento
mileage
milieu

millennium
millionaire
miniature
minor
minuscule
minutiae
misapprehension
miscellaneous
mischievous
missile
misspell
morale
mortgage
movable
mysterious
naturally
necessary
negotiate
neither
nevertheless
nickel
noticeable
nowadays
nuclear
nuisance
numerous
obsolescent
obstacle
occasion
occurrence
offense
omission
omitted
oneself
opinion
opponent
opportunity
opposite
oppression
optimism

ordinance
ordinarily
originally
outrageous
pamphlet
panicky
parallel
partially
particularly
pastime
patience
peaceable
peculiar
penetrate
perceive
performance
perhaps
permanent
permissible
perquisite
perseverance
persistent
personnel
perspective
perspiration
persuade
phase
phenomenon
phony
physical
plagiarism
planned
plausible
pleasant
politician
pollute
possession
possibly
practically
prairie

precedence

precipice

predominantly

preferred

prejudice

preparation

prerequisite

prerogative

presumptuous

pretense

prevail

prevalent

preventive

primitive

principle

privilege

probably

procedure

proceed

process

professor

programmed

prohibition

prominent

promissory

pronunciation

propaganda

propeller

prophecy

prospective

psychiatric

psychological

publicly

pursue

quandary

quantity

quarrel

questionnaire

queue

quizzes

rarefy

rarity

receipt

receive

recession

recipe

recipient

recognize

recommend

reconnaissance

reconnoiter

recruit

recyclable

reference

referring

regrettable

regular

rehearsal

reinforce

relevant

relief

relieve

religious

remembrance

reminisce

renaissance

renowned

repellant

repetition

rescind

resemblance

resistance

restaurant

retroactive

rhapsody

rhetorical

rhyme

rhythm

ridiculous

roommate

sacrifice

sacrilegious

safety

salable

salvage

satellite

scarcity

scenery

schedule

scissors

secede

secretary

seize

separate

sergeant

several

severely

shepherd

shining

shrubbery

siege

signaled

significant

similar

simultaneous

sincerely

sizable

skeptic

skiing

skillful

soliloquy

sophomore

souvenir

spacious

specimen

specious

speech

sponsor

stationery

statistics

straight
stratagem
strategy
strength
strenuous
stretch
strictly
studying
subpoena
subtlety
suburban
succeed
succession
suggest
suing
summary
superintendent
supersede
suppress
surely
surgeon
surprise
surreptitious
surround
surveillance
susceptible
suspicious
synonymous

tariff
technique
temperament
temperature
temporary
tempt
theater
theory
therefore
thorough
though
threshold
tobacco
totaled
tragedy
transferable
traveled
tremendous
truly
typical
tyranny
unanimous
unconscious
unctuous
undoubtedly
unforgettable
unfortunately
unique

unmanageable
unnecessary
unusual
unwieldy
usage
usually
vacillate
vacuum
various
vegetable
vengeance
villain
violence
visible
volume
warehouse
warrant
warring
weather
weird
whether
whichever
wholly
wield
woeful
yield

See also: SIMILAR WORDS

*   *   *

Style and Tone

Choices writers make in the way they express ideas are style decisions. The result is the tone of a document. The nature of the document and the intended audience dictate the style; the style decisions create the tone. The two are impossible to distinguish and should be studied together.

1. Select the style with the audience in mind.

A formal letter, report, or proposal should have a completely different style and tone than a personal note, memo, or internal newsletter.

> *An informal note:*
> Hey, Bob, did you hear that McGee was promoted to vice president? I'll always remember him as the guy who was in front of the losing team at the company picnic's tug-of-war—all covered with mud!

> *Company newsletter:*
> Mark McGee was promoted to vice president of operations this month. Congratulations, Mark. We'll always remember your leadership at the company picnic; now we'll see how you do with a window office.

> *Press release:*
> ANCO Corporation announced this morning the promotion of Mark McGee to vice president of operations. McGee, an employee of 12 years, was formerly manager of the Operations Department.

All three styles are different, and all are appropriate for the audience to which they are addressed. Everyone alters style depending on the audience, and the resulting tone of a communication reflects those decisions.

2. Edit for tone as well as mechanics.

Most people associate editing with sentence structure, spelling, punctuation, and arrangement of material. Those are important editing points, but they are only the basics of good writing. Edit yourself for tone as well. Be aware that sometimes subtle writing decisions affect tone dramatically.

Preedited formal message:
> We ask that you consider our proposal seriously. We can do the job and would appreciate the chance to work with you and prove it. This is just the kind of project we are capable of.

Postedited formal message:
> We hope you will consider our proposal. We are confident of our ability to provide the highest quality work, and we look forward to the opportunity of working with you.

The second version is stronger and more direct, and it avoids the use of uncertainty or a weak message. The first version weakly asks the reader to "consider our proposal seriously." The improved tone of the second version, in which the writer hopes "you will consider our proposal," is only slightly different; however, it has more confidence, is more direct, and conveys a sense of professionalism.

3. Select words carefully to improve style.

Business writing demands extreme diplomacy in many cases, and the method selected to convey an idea can make a vast difference in the response. Three different methods follow.

Emotional:
> I am so angry about your actions that I could scream.
> Believe me, the day will come when you need a favor

> from this department, and I won't forget the way you
> have treated me.

Discreet:

> I am perplexed. We have worked together on many
> occasions, always with satisfactory results. No doubt,
> we will have to work together in the future. I would
> have preferred a constructive dialogue with you, so that
> we might feel free to provide assistance to you as we
> have done in the past.

Formal:

> We were deeply concerned at the recent misunder-
> standing. I remain convinced, however, that
> constructive dialogue is still possible, and I suggest a
> conciliatory meeting at your earliest convenience.

4. Vary sentence and paragraph length.

Sentence and paragraph length determine reader interest and comprehension. Paragraphs in lengthy documents make a visual impression on the reader. If they all look about the same in length (especially if all are long), the document will seem formidable and uninteresting, even before the reader attempts to read it. If those sentences vary in length, the visual impression is more pleasing.

The same argument can be made for sentence length. If all sentences are about the same length, they are monotonous, like a steady drumbeat in the reader's ear. The monotony destroys reader interest almost as soon as the problem presents itself.

Sentences of similar length:

> We need to meet next week to review the preliminary
> budget. Several problems have been pointed out in the
> document. We will need to prepare a complete revision
> before submitting it. We have also failed to provide
> adequate supporting documentation. As it is, we cannot
> justify the expense levels we have projected. I suggest we
> meet at your office on Monday or Tuesday, if convenient.

Sentences of varied length:

> We need to meet next week to review the preliminary budget. Several problems need fixing. For example, some expense levels appear unacceptable and have to be revised. We also overlooked documenting our assumptions. Let's take another look at the whole thing at your office on Monday or Tuesday.

5. Choose a format to make the best impression.

The style chosen for letters, reports, memos, newsletters, and proposals determines how they are received. The appearance of such documents makes an important first impression, and the importance of style decisions should not be overlooked. The following basic standards should always be followed:

- Every document leaving the company should look completely professional in every way.
- Check all spelling on every document, and correct all errors before the final draft.
- On all documents, provide enough "white space" on each page so that readers will not be overwhelmed by the text.
- Apply decisions about punctuation, margins, indentations, and other mechanics consistently within a single document.
- Be sure employees always edit their own work for tone, seeking the right words and phrases for the circumstances. Encourage employees to work with one another for constructive criticism of style and tone.
- Ensure that department managers establish minimum standards for style and tone of communications leaving the department, and institute procedures to ensure that these guidelines are followed.

See also: ACTIVE AND PASSIVE VOICE; CLICHÉS; DENOTATION AND CONNOTATION; EDITING AND PROOFREADING; JARGON

*   *   *

SUMMARIZING

The ability to summarize critical information is essential in business. The readership for the array of reports, proposals, memos, letters, and other documents is able to devote only a limited amount of time to each piece of paper crossing the desk. A summary enables the reader to determine quickly what the document is all about, why it is important, and whether it is necessary to read further.

1. Decide exactly what has to be summarized.

Make a distinction between a summary and an abstract. An *abstract* briefly summarizes the topics included in a document; a *summary* concentrates on the primary conclusion or point. For example, an abstract of a research article includes a range of points, intended to advise the reader of the range of topics covered in the entire article. A summary of the same article would list primary conclusions or the main point of revelation.

2. Select an appropriate format for the summary.

The traditional method of placing summaries at the end of documents is ineffective. Rather, the most crucial facts should be presented at the beginning. Summarize as succinctly as possible. If it is necessary to expand on a simple statement, introduce the point and then provide a short listing of critical conclusions.

The summary should always fit on one page (or it is not truly a summary)—and preferably in a single paragraph. Remember that the purpose is to enable the reader to understand what is included in the entire document in as short a time as possible. The more briefly this can be said in the summary, the more successful the effort.

3. Consider sending a summary only as a first step.

Some documents might not be of interest to everyone on a distribution list. In this instance, a summary can represent a one-page invitation to request a copy of the longer document. This will save printing and distribution expense, as well as time, and will mean more efficient use of file space, manual or automated.

4. Begin lengthy reports with a summary page.

Virtually all reports will be more effective if they start with a one-page summary. The summary page should explain:

- The purpose of the report
- The major conclusion or recommendation
- Financial considerations (cost and savings)
- Deadlines or implementation points

5. Always start proposals with the bottom line.

Assuming a proposal is an offer to perform work or a recommendation for a change in procedures within the organization, the reader is virtually always interested in the conclusion. A summary achieves this. The proposal can be constructed in four sections: (1) a single-page summary, (2) an expanded introduction introducing the issues, (3) the body of the report and conclusions of any studies or other materials, and (4) a supplement including any lengthy statistical information.

6. Write letters beginning with a summary of the most important part.

Follow the opening with a detailed discussion, and end with another summary. The initial paragraph of the letter should get the reader's interest and attention, and make the reader want to read the whole letter. Think of the business letter as an opening and closing summary, with the details sandwiched in between.

See also: Introductions; Letters; Reports

*   *   *

Table of Contents

A Table of Contents is necessary in any document longer than eight to ten pages. It gives the reader a frame of reference for finding major sections of the report and indicates the scope and coverage of the report.

1.   Use the table of contents as an outline to organize work and the sequence and contents of the report.

In organizing the document, convert an initial outline to sequence guideline, and ultimately to a Table of Contents.

2.   Decide how much detail to include in the table based on the nature of the report.

If the report has only a few sections but they are long, include all major subsections with page number in the Table of Contents. Indent subheads so readers know where chapter or section breaks occur.

3.   Coordinate all references in the Table of Contents.

Chapter numbers should be the same as those used for each chapter, and numbering systems should be the same. Apply this rule to chapter numbers as well as to subheads.

4.   Place one-page summaries before the Table of Contents.

If you are beginning your document with a one-page summary, place the summary after the title page but before the Table of Contents. Refer to the summary by a lowercase roman numeral, and number the Table of Contents with roman numerals as well. Begin arabic lettering with the main body of the report.

5.   Use leader lines to connect section headings to page numbers.

Although the use of leader lines is optional, it draws the reader's attention to the fact that it is a Table of Contents.

Sample Table of Contents:

*   *   *

Technical Writing

Any organization involved with technical matters faces the constant problem of internal communication. The company invariably is divided into two groups: the technicians and the administrators. This becomes a problem whenever the technical side is required to communicate with the administrative, especially when dealing with matters of budgets, projects, commitments of capital, or marketing.

1. Take all steps necessary to facilitate communication between technical and nontechnical employees.

Develop a glossary for nontechnical employees to use, so that essential terms can be understood by both sides.

2. Use a nontechnical writer to work with the technical experts.

A common mistake is to use technical style and language for reports aimed at a nontechnical audience. Too many technical writers write only for fellow experts. When reports must go outside the technical arena, communication is always difficult. The problems should be addressed at the draft phase rather than during a presentation meeting. The use of a nontechnical writer makes sense in these situations.

3. Label reports carefully and provide footnotes to explain important terminology.

Follow the general guidelines for report preparation. Highly detailed information should be included by way of appendix material, while the body of a report should concentrate on primary issues: the cost and benefit of an idea to the company, the need for changes in procedures, compliance with regulatory reporting requirements, or nontechnical recommendations for the technical department, for example.

4. Follow the universal guidelines for reports, letters, proposals, and other document production.

Even in the most technical application, readers will not always be technicians. The most effective report makes a clear case for an issue without isolating nontechnical readers.

5. Avoid technical style within the report, especially if the primary audience is nontechnical.

Reports that are passed around just among technical employees can be written at a high level; however, the writing style for most reports should avoid unnecessarily complicated language.

Unedited statement:
> The primary purpose of the study was to observe data concerning operation of the newly designed equipment and to test assumptions in a simulated environment, thus providing the means for recommended improvements in subsequent prototypes.

Edited statement:
> We conducted the study to test the newly designed equipment in a simulated environment, so that we could recommend improvements in the design.

See also: Style and Tone

*　*　*

TITLES

Business writing is typified by examples of titles. Individuals, organizations, references to published material, and government agencies are found in most types of business correspondence.

1. Follow the correct format for publication names and titles.

The title of a book, newspaper, or magazine is italicized or underlined. The title of an article or a book chapter is placed within quotation marks. Provide the volume or date of publication for newspapers and magazines, and the place and year of publication for books.

Examples:
> "Producing the Business Newsletter." *Business Times Magazine* 31 (April 1996).
> "Inventory Alternatives." *Spokane Word,* May 12, 1996, pp. 12–13.
> *Budgeting for the 21st Century.* Buffalo, N.Y.: Business Press, 1996.

2. Identify proper methods for identifying people by name and title.

If an individual has a special title, use it in place of the usual *Mr.* or *Ms.* The first time a name is mentioned in a letter or report, use the title and full name; abbreviate subsequent references.

Examples:
> Ms. Harmon and Dr. Green arrived today at our corporate headquarters office. Following lunch, Ms. Harmon gave a speech to the board of directors, and Dr. Green went into a private meeting with the CEO.
> Chief Financial Officer Harold Carter advised the finance committee that current forecasts were inaccurate. Carter

said that until being appointed CFO, he had never seen such an unwillingness by management to face reality.

3.   Use full titles upon first mention only.

When a person is first mentioned, precede the name with the full title, with the first letter of major title words capitalized. Subsequently, only the last name needs to be given.

Example:

Chief Executive Officer Maria Polmar has released the latest quarter's results. Polmar pointed out that several extraordinary items have distorted the profit picture, and she predicted a healthy third quarter.

4.   Do not capitalize titles when they are referred to without a specific person's name attached to them.

Example:

Virtually every chief financial officer in the survey responded that education was not the key factor. Several agreed that vice presidents and senior managers in organizations have more hands-on impact than the president, whose task is to provide overall guidance.

5.   Treat organization and agency names, schools, and association names as proper nouns.

Capitalize the first letter of each key word.

Examples:

Eastman Kodak
Department of the Interior
Harvard University
Rotary Club

See also: CITATIONS

*   *   *

TRANSITIONS

A transition is a bridge between one thought and another that smooths out the flow of thought. Just as a conversation moves from topic to topic without discernable changes, the written word requires transitions to lead the reader from one idea to the next.

1. Restrict paragraphs to a single idea to make sentence-to-sentence transitions easy.

Transitions from sentence to sentence within a paragraph are relatively easy, since the paragraph should be restricted to one major idea. Even the beginning writer usually has little trouble with natural transitions, the natural connection between fragments of a primary thought represented by a series of related sentences. Most writers run into problems when they end a paragraph and move to the next one.

2. Work to achieve smooth transitions between paragraphs.

Transitions between paragraphs require some thought. Because paragraph endings signal the resting of one idea and the beginning of another, transition is not always natural or easy.

> *Paragraphs lacking transition:*
> The organizational requirements for putting together a company newsletter make all the difference between a highly effective, current report, and a mere collection of stories.
> When selecting a printer, be sure to ask critical questions. Not every printing company operates in the same manner, and cost as well as quality considerations matter greatly.

Where will you find your stories? This is always the main question on the mind of the first-time newsletter editor. Do not worry. Finding stories worthy of your newsletter will be the least of your concerns.

Paragraphs with transition:

The organizational requirements for putting together a company newsletter make all the difference between a highly effective, current report and a mere collection of stories.

The first step in organizing your new venture is finding the right printer. Be sure to ask critical questions. Not every printing company operates in the same manner, and cost as well as quality considerations matter greatly.

Of course, even with the most economical printing source, you still need to locate and write interesting copy. Where will you find your stories? This is always the main question on the mind of the first-time newsletter editor. Do not worry. Finding stories worthy of your newsletter will be the least of your concerns.

With only minor changes, the paragraphs now flow smoothly from one thought to another. The transition is nothing more than a bridge between thoughts, as the above example illustrates.

3.   Use comparisons and contrasting thoughts to keep writing lively and conversational.

Readers like to have ideas introduced by way of comparison and contrast. With these devices, reading is not merely a lecture of ideas; it becomes a lively demonstration.

Paragraphs lacking comparison or contrast:

An effective budget depends on careful coordination between last year's actual experience and your expectations for the coming year. Learn from your mistakes.

Don't simply view mistakes as failures. They are learning devices and you can improve the budgeting

process for each expense account by keeping track of
what occurred in last year's budget. Improve based on
what you learned.

There is nothing wrong with the style or message of these paragraphs. They are easily understood and the intended message comes through clearly. However, the style and transition are not particularly imaginative or illustrative.

Paragraphs with comparison or contrast:

An effective budget depends on careful coordination
between last year's actual experience and your
expectations for the coming year. Just as a new driver
dents a few fenders, anyone who prepares a budget
should be ready to learn from his or her mistakes.

If you backed into another car the first time you tried
to park, you wouldn't give up and determine never to
drive. Budgeting is the same way. Don't simply view
mistakes as failures. They are learning devices, and you
can improve the budgeting process for each expense
account by keeping track of what occurred in last year's
budget. Improve based on what you learned; and watch
out for other traffic along your budgeting highway.

4. Avoid easy tricks to achieve transition.

Don't try to get around creative transitions by using devices, such as obvious connecting words or repeating the previous paragraph's concluding idea. Readers see through these techniques and consider such writing to be lazy and ineffective.

Transition with connecting words:

The site inspection is essential as a first step in
organizing a company seminar. Be sure to invest the time
in examining the hotel, meeting room, and catering
facilities in advance, and meet with the sales manager to
arrange for essential services.

However, when your guests arrive on the first day of
the convention, a number of problems will arise, not all of
them anticipated. Be sure you have made arrangements
with the hotel for receiving shipments, in case attendees

and speakers instruct their home offices to send material
to their attention. Too often, essential materials are
misplaced because a marketing manager forgot to speak
with the front desk.

Notice that the transition between the two paragraphs is not a
real one. These are two completely different topics, and the use
of *however* does not make a real transition.

A better transition:

The site inspection is essential as a first step in
organizing a company seminar. Be sure to invest the time
in examining the hotel, meeting room, and catering
facilities in advance, and meet with the sales manager to
arrange for essential services.

Advance preparation is the key. However, you
cannot anticipate every possible problem that will arise,
even with the most detailed advance inspection. When
guests arrive on the first day of the convention, a number
of problems will arise, not all of them anticipated. Be sure
you have made arrangements with the hotel for receiving
shipments, in case attendees and speakers instruct their
home offices to send material to their attention. Too often,
essential materials are misplaced because a marketing
manager forgot to speak with the front desk.

In this improved version, a single sentence creates a bridge between the two paragraphs.

Transitions are not difficult; they often require only a little
thought to make the flow of communication effective and enjoya-
ble for the reader.

5.   Use consequence, generalization, diver-
sion, and other conversational tools to
achieve smooth transitions.

These useful devices should be kept in mind not as methods to
use to avoid real transition work but to aid in the construction
of the idea.

Consequence:

> The business meeting should always begin on time.
> Announce this as a policy and do all you can to enforce it, and attendees will soon realize that it is in everyone's interest to show up at the announced time.
> Be cautious, though. The president of the company might not appreciate being chewed out for being two minutes late to *your* meeting. There are probably countless reasons why even the best-run meetings will start late now and then.

Generalization:

> The difficult, confrontive employee presents a special challenge to every manager. Such situations take up a lot of time and thought, while producing little in the way of productive result.
> In the majority of such cases, the problems can be largely defused by recognizing that the employee may be bored with his or her work assignments. Look for ways to expand the range of tasks, and many of those problems will dissipate as a result.

Diversion:

> Asking the boss for a raise is never a pleasant task. You need to think ahead and come up with good, solid, business-related reasons to justify the request. Financial need is *not* a good reason. Point to examples of how you have saved money by reducing expenses or streamlining procedures as evidence of your value to the company.
> By the way, an especially good time to make such a request is following several months of balancing your department's budget. Be prepared to show some hard and fast numbers demonstrating not only that you are valuable but that you know your worth.

6.   Use illustrative transition.

Make your writing sparkle by using effective and practical illustrations. This is an especially effective tool for business writing, because it lends power to a point the writer is trying to make. Business readers expect to be presented with facts, and the illustrative transition is probably the best way to get your point across.

Illustrative transition:

> Our recommendation for the purchase of equipment will require an initial capital investment of $30,000. However, we expect to recapture the entire cost in less than one year. From that point forward, reduced labor costs will save the company more than $2,500 per month.
>
> That translates to an offset equal to budget increases in Salary and Wage expenses for the previous six quarters in this department. These estimates are based on utilization by one shift only. If the procedure were put into place for all three shifts, the division could increase its labor force by 15 percent and still operate at today's cost level.

In this example, the main point is made in the first paragraph, but the illustration in the second paragraph, while providing a transition, also provides valuable and convincing arguments.

See also: PARAGRAPHS; STYLE AND TONE

*   *   *

WORD PROCESSING

The range of functions performed by desk computers, aimed at creating, manipulating, storing, and printing text, are referred to generally as *word processing*. The term is not accurate today, however. In their original form, word processing systems were expensive, awkward, and extremely limited. Today, the combination of text files with graphics, along with modem transmission of all types of files, merges, and e-mail, have made word processing an efficient and inexpensive device for managing virtually all forms of business communication.

1. Learn the system thoroughly.

Every word processing system has its own special features and quirks. More and more, however, systems are becoming standardized. Today, a fairly inexpensive system provides the ability to alter fonts, type sizes, and spacing and to format documents in a variety of ways. The better a user understands the potential and limits of a system, the more valuable it becomes.

2. Set up formats that can be used repeatedly for similar documents.

Even a document as simple as a letter or memo should follow some basic formatting rules. Set up a blank file with the margins, tabs, top and bottom spacing, headers (if applicable), and other needed features. Use that file repeatedly to set up other files with the same template formatting.

3. Work from standard formats used universally by your organization.

Before setting up a template file for letters or memos, find out whether your organization has published guidelines for such documents. If it had, be sure to coordinate your format file with the procedural requirements.

4. Use the functions that are provided with the system.

Functions such as proofing, grammar check, and thesaurus are valuable features and should be used to improve manuscript format as well as writing style. Proofing is a fast and efficient feature, available with a single keystroke. You usually have to place the cursor at the beginning of the document, because the system will probably begin proofing from the point the command is entered. Most proofing programs allow several choices when a word appears that is not in the computer dictionary.

You can indicate the word is okay, add the word to the dictionary, enter a correction, or ask for a list of suggested spellings of words close to the spelling in the file. Such programs also question repeated sequential words.

A grammar-check program points out inconsistencies in grammar within a document. Be cautious in using this feature, however. In some cases, style should overrule strictly correct grammatical decisions. Use the grammar check feature to find obvious errors of grammar, but maintain the right to make style judgments as well.

The thesaurus is a useful feature for expanding a vocabulary or for finding the right word. Type in a word with the face meaning, and check the thesaurus. All words with similar or identical meanings are listed; pick the one you like and, with a keystroke, it replaces the one in the document.

5.   Save files often, and back up your files.

Every computer manual gives this advice, and everyone training someone on a computer repeats it. Saving and making backup copies of files are easy routines, but they are too often overlooked or ignored as procedural matters. Hours of hard work can be lost in a split second, often for unexplained reasons. Files can and do vanish for no apparent reason. If they are not recoverable, the data could be lost forever.

6.   Label files so they can be found quickly and easily.

If you write letters to one person on a regular basis, it makes sense to label a file with that person's name, within a path labeled "letters." If you have a large number of files, be especially careful to provide names that will make sense when you go looking for them later. If your system provides a description box as part of the file name, use it. This convenient feature makes locating files easier later on.

7.   Purge old files periodically.

If you are not sure whether you can get rid of a series of files, copy them onto a diskette and erase them from the hard disk. Old files take up disk space and slow down the processing speed of the system. The more files there are, the longer every search takes, and the more tedious the task becomes of storing, retrieving, saving, and replacing files.

8.   Make backup copies when working on revisions.

Always keep a backup copy, especially when providing copies for other people to revise. If you work on projects with others, a draft copy of a document can be saved to a diskette and sent to someone else for additional changes. Always make a backup copy, for a number of reasons. First, the other person might lose or accidentally erase your file. Second, the scope of changes might be extensive but wrong; you may need to refer to the original form of the document. Third, some people will change some parts of a document while erasing sections they don't think are essential but that *are* essential. Don't assume that others will use common sense or ask before they erase.

9.   Before your final draft, proofread on hard copy.

Even when people are accustomed to working on screens, editing is not that easy. Proofread on a printed draft before finalizing the document.

Sample
Forms
Section

BUDGET FORM

	Jan.	Feb.	Mar.	Apr.	May	Jun.	Jul.	Aug.	Sep.	Oct.	Nov.	Dec.	Total
Office Supplies													
Telephone													
Rent													
Salaries and Wages													
Payroll Taxes													
Benefit Programs													
Dues & Subscriptions													
Maintenance													
Cleaning													
Entertainment													
Travel													
Automotive Expenses													
Advertising													
Promotion													
Conventions													
Professional Fees													
Taxes													
Licenses and Fees													
Miscellaneous													
Total													

BUDGET DOCUMENTATION

Account _____ Year _____

Assumptions _____

_____

Assumption Categories (see explanation below)

Month	A	B	C	D	E	Total
Jan						
Feb						
Mar						
Apr						
May						
Jun						
Jul						
Aug						
Sep						
Oct						
Nov						
Dec						
Total						

Explanations:

A_____

B_____

C_____

D_____

E_____

BUDGET VARIANCE SUMMARY

Company Name

Month _____

	Current Month				Year to Date			
	Actual	Budget	Variance	%	Actual	Budget	Variance	%
Account								
Office Supplies								
Telephone								
Rent								
Salaries and Wages								
Payroll Taxes								
Benefit Programs								
Dues & Subscriptions								
Maintenance								
Cleaning								
Entertainment								
Travel								
Automotive Expenses								
Advertising								
Promotion								
Conventions								
Professional Fees								
Taxes								
Licenses and Fees								
Miscellaneous								
Total								

FORECAST

Line of business or source of revenues

Month	A	B	C	D	Total
January					
February					
March					
April					
May					
June					
July					
August					
September					
October					
November					
December					
TOTAL					

Line of business or source of revenue:

A_____

B_____

C_____

D_____

BALANCE SHEET

Sample Corporation
Balance Sheet
December 31, 1997, and December 31, 1996

	12-31-97	12-31-96
Current Assets:		
Cash	$ 8,213	$ 6,156
Accounts Receivable	55,007	75,215
Inventory	134,600	199,050
Total Current Assets	$197,820	$280,421
Fixed Assets:		
Furniture	$107,240	$107,240
Machinery and Equipment	12,682	4,214
Real Estate	392,800	325,000
	$512,722	$436,454
Less: Accumulated Depreciation	107,250	92,015
Net Fixed Assets	$405,472	$344,439
Total Assets	$603,292	$624,860
Current Liabilities:		
Accounts Payable	$ 13,411	$ 15,410
Taxes Payable	6,004	4,881
Current Portion, Notes Payable	115,219	115,219
Total Current Liabilities	$134,219	$135,510
Long-Term Liabilities:		
Long-Term Notes Payable	$217,500	$237,004
Total Liabilities	$352,134	$372,514
Net Worth:		
Capital Stock	$100,000	$100,000
Retained Earnings	151,158	152,346
Total Net Worth	$251,158	$252,346
Total Liabilities and Net Worth	$603,292	$624,860

INCOME STATEMENT

Sample Corporation
Income Statement
For the Twelve-Month Periods Ending
January 1, 1997, and December 31, 1996

	1-1-97 to 12-31-97	1-1-96 to 12-31-96
Gross Sales	$1,814,266	$1,600,218
Cost of Goods Sold:		
Inventory, January 1	$ 199,050	$ 174,451
Purchases	704,290	715,872
Direct Labor	153,288	97,403
	$1,056,628	$ 987,726
Less: Inventory, December 31	134,600	$ 199,050
Cost of Goods Sold	$ 922,028	$ 788,676
Gross Profit	$ 892,238	$ 811,542
Total Expenses*	$ 893,426	$ 803,213
Net Profit (Loss) (Difference between gross profit and total expenses)	$ (1,188)	$ 8,329

* Refer to the itemized list on the following page.

Expenses:

Depreciation	$ 15,235	$ 13,419
Office Supplies	4,218	3,186
Telephone	9,466	7,004
Rent	48,015	41,416
Salaries and Wages	532,415	482,007
Payroll Taxes	61,210	51,615
Benefit Programs	78,016	72,015
Dues and Subscriptions	11,415	9,157
Maintenance	13,707	8,006
Cleaning	4,915	2,847
Entertainment	2,110	2,915
Travel	13,263	8,817
Automotive Expenses	8,800	6,224
Advertising	38,960	34,484
Promotion	13,286	18,014
Conventions	9,004	17,725
Professional Fees	16,500	16,211
Taxes	1,996	708
Licenses and Fees	4,018	4,226
Miscellaneous	6,877	3,217

STATEMENT OF CASH FLOWS

Sample Corporation
Statement of Cash Flows
For the Twelve-Month Periods Ending
January 1, 1997, and December 31, 1996

	1-1-97 to 12-31-97	1-1-96 to 12-31-96
Sources of Funds:		
Net Profit (Loss)	$ (1,188)	$ 8,329
Plus: Non-cash expense, Depreciation	15,235	$ 13,419
Total Sources of Funds	$ 14,047	$ 21,748
Applications of Funds:		
Acquisition of Fixed Assets	$ 76,268	$ 12,516
Reduction of Long-Term Liabilities	19,504	13,005
Total Applications of Funds	$ (81,725)	$ (3,873)
Changes in Cash Flows:		
Cash	$ 2,057	$ (1,136)
Accounts Receivable	(20,208)	12,005
Inventory	(64,450)	(16,215)
Accounts Payable	1,999	659
Taxes Payable	(1,123)	814
Net Increase (Decrease) in Cash Flows	$ (81,725)	$ (3,873)

Note: Total applications of funds always match net increase (decrease) in cash flows.

LETTERS

Block Style

May 16, 1997

Robert Simmons, Vice President
Midwest General Merchandise Co.
Varna, IL 61375

Re: New line of hardware

Dear Mr. Simmons:

Thank you for your detailed summary concerning the market potential for the new product line we are developing. As one of our highest-volume customers, your opinion was valuable.

Your observation that geographic exclusive rights agreements might be worthwhile is particularly interesting. However, we would also want to develop some idea of the proposed volume of business we might expect from your stores.

I will receive a staff report May 23, and I will call you then to discuss a mutually advantageous strategy.

Sincerely,

Harold March, President

cc: Sharon Handley

encl.

Modified Block Style

May 16, 1997

Robert Simmons, Vice President
Midwest General Merchandise Co.
Varna, IL 61375

Re: New line of hardware

Dear Mr. Simmons:

Thank you for your detailed summary concerning the market potential for the new product line we are developing. As one of our highest-volume customers, your opinion was of great interest to us.

We have studied numerous alternatives in considering how to proceed. Your observation that geographic exclusive rights agreements might be worthwhile is particularly interesting. However, we would also want to develop some idea of the proposed and likely volume of business we might expect from your stores. As you pointed out, the savings in promotional, shipping, and fulfillment would enable us to provide you with the merchandise at a reduced cost. We agree, and this should be factored in to our analysis.

Our marketing division is taking another look at the overall plan with your suggestions in mind. We plan to have the report by May 23. I will telephone you by the end of that week and let you know what we have decided.

I hope that we will be able to work out a mutually satisfactory marketing arrangement.

Sincerely,

Harold March, President

cc. Sharon Handley

encl.

Semiblock Style

May 16, 1997

Robert Simmons, Vice President
Midwest General Merchandise Co.
Varna, IL 61375

Re: New line of hardware

Dear Mr. Simmons:

Thank you for your detailed summary concerning the market potential for the new product line we are developing. As one of our highest-volume customers, your opinion was of great interest to us.

We have studied numerous alternatives in considering how to proceed. Your observation that geographic exclusive rights agreements might be worthwhile is particularly interesting. However, we would also want to develop some idea of the proposed and likely volume of business we might expect from your stores. As you pointed out, the savings in promotional, shipping, and fulfillment would enable us to provide you with the merchandise at a reduced cost. We agree, and this should be factored in to our analysis.

Our marketing division is taking another look at the overall plan with your suggestions in mind. We plan to have the report by May 23. I will telephone you by the end of that week and let you know what we have decided.

I hope that we will be able to work out a mutually satisfactory marketing arrangement.

Sincerely,

Harold March, President

cc. Sharon Handley

encl.

LONG-RANGE PLANNING DOCUMENTS

Objective Statement Worksheet

a. Management
b. Internal staff
c. Vendors and suppliers
d. Customers
e. Other (regulatory agencies, etc.)

Important elements of the objective:

professional management and staff
high morale
vendors considered as important as customers
customer satisfaction a must
within regulatory rules

Objective statement:

This organization employs the most qualified management and staff, works toward maintaining high staff morale, and recognizes the absolute need for vendor, supplier,
and customer satisfaction, in order to provide the best
service and to comply with the law while doing so.

Goals and Identification of Goals

Program (or department) <u>Marketing Department</u>

Goals:

GOAL 1 <u>Improve average productivity of sales reps.</u>
DEADLINE <u>12/31</u>
MEASURE OF SUCCESS <u>Monthly monitoring; incentive program; termination of chronic under-performing reps.</u>

GOAL 2 <u>Increase number of weekly calls by 15%</u>
DEADLINE <u>3/31</u>
MEASURE OF SUCCESS <u>Weekly sales call report review; compliance with procedure mandatory</u>

GOAL 3 <u>Lower nonessential overhead level</u>
DEADLINE <u>2/28</u>
MEASURE OF SUCCESS <u>Monthly budget review; improved internal controls</u>

MEMORANDUM

To: Bob Simmons

From: Hal March

Date: 5/16/97

Re: New line of hardware

Thanks for the detailed summary concerning market potential for our new product line. We really appreciate your input.

We've been looking at several alternatives and haven't made a final decision yet. We were interested, though, in your idea about exclusive rights on a geographic basis. It would be valuable for you to write up an estimate of the volume of business you expect to generate, were you to get an exclusive. We agree with your point that promotional, shipping, and fulfillment costs would be relatively low, and we plan to factor that in to our final analysis.

I've asked the marketing division to take another look at this whole thing, with your ideas in mind. They have promised to get the report to me by May 23, and you and I should talk by telephone by the end of that week. By then, I should be able to tell you how we've decided to proceed.

I hope it works out so that your marketing ideas are included in the final plan.

Sample Page From Procedures Manual

12.03.00   Customer Service Report

12.03.05   This report is generated in the Customer Response Department at the end of each week. It contains a summary of the previous five business days' customer contacts, by both telephone and mail.

12.03.10   Format of the report: The report is a summary and survey. It reports the following information:
            —date of contact (range by week)
            —breakdown of telephone and mail contacts by day and number
            —identification of product line and/or department involved
            —category of complaint by twelve separate broad types

12.03.15   Distribution: The report is sent via interoffice mail to all department heads, the marketing vice president, and the president.

12.03.20   Related reports: The department performs a follow-up survey of all customers registering a complaint with the department. This survey, conducted by telephone, is designed to determine whether the customer was satisfied by the response received, its timeliness, and whether the customer intends to continue shopping at our stores.

12.03.25　　Distribution of related reports: The follow-up survey is sent with most recent Customer Service Reports to the same distribution list.

12.03.30　　Sample forms: Samples of all documents and forms are attached.

CSD / rev. 12/96

INDEX